STORYFUN 3

TEACHER'S BOOK

Second edition

Karen Saxby

Emily Hird

Cambridge University Press
www.cambridge.org/elt

Cambridge Assessment English
www.cambridgeenglish.org

Information on this title: www.cambridge.org/9781316617182

© Cambridge University Press 2017

It is normally necessary for written permission for copying to be obtained in advance from a publisher. The worksheets at the back of this book are designed to be copied and distributed in class. The normal requirements are waived here and it is not necessary to write to Cambridge University Press for permission for an individual teacher to make copies for use within his or her own classroom. Only those pages which carry the wording **'PHOTOCOPIABLE © Cambridge University Press 2017'** may be copied.

First published 2011
Second edition 2017

20 19 18 17 16 15 14 13 12 11 10 9 8

Printed in Great Britain by CPI Group (UK) Ltd, Croydon CR0 4YY

A catalogue record for this publication is available from the British Library

ISBN 978-1-316-61715-1 Student's Book with online activities and Home Fun booklet 3
ISBN 978-1-316-61718-2 Teacher's Book with Audio 3
ISBN 978-1-316-61721-2 Presentation plus 3

Cambridge University Press has no responsibility for the persistence or accuracy of URLs for external or third-party internet websites referred to in this publication, and does not guarantee that any content on such websites is, or will remain, accurate or appropriate. Information regarding prices, travel timetables and other factual information given in this work is correct at the time of first printing but Cambridge University Press does not guarantee the accuracy of such information thereafter.

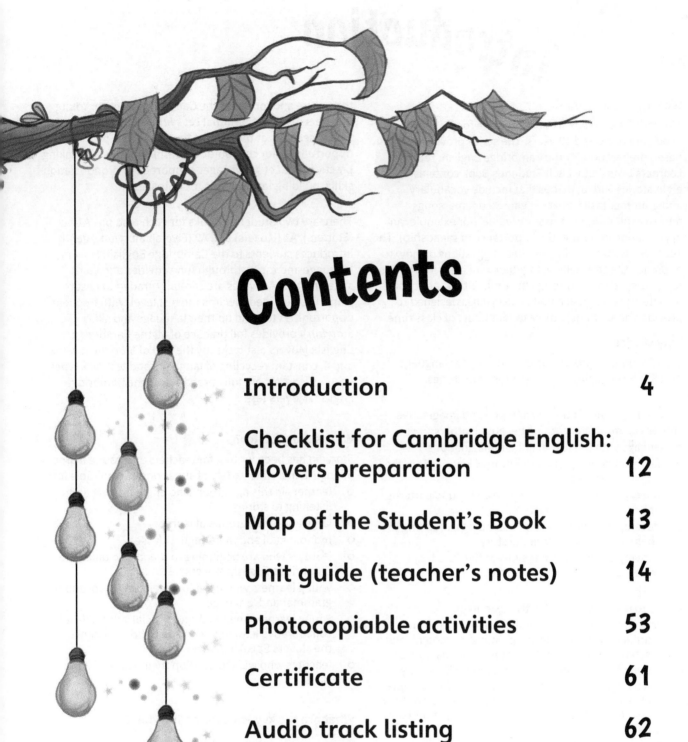

Contents

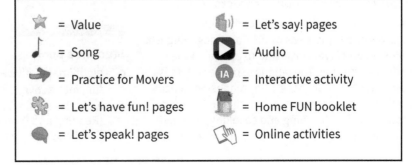

☆ = Value

♪ = Song

➜ = Practice for Movers

✳ = Let's have fun! pages

💬 = Let's speak! pages

🔊 = Let's say! pages

▶ = Audio

IA = Interactive activity

🏠 = Home FUN booklet

✍ = Online activities

Introduction

Welcome to *Storyfun*!

Storyfun is a series of six books written for young learners aged between 6 and 12 years. The series provides story-based preparation for the Cambridge English: Young Learners tests (YLE). Each Student's Book contains eight stories with activities that include vocabulary and grammar tasks, puzzles, games, poems, songs and an exploration of the story 'value' (for example, an appreciation of nature, the importance of friendship). The Teacher's Books provide detailed suggestions on how to approach the storytelling, together with clear instructions for guiding learners through the unit. With a variety of flexible resources, each unit in *Storyfun* is designed to provide approximately three to four hours of class time.

Why stories?

Storyfun aims to provide an opportunity for language practice by engaging learners' interest in stories.

Research has shown that meaningful and imaginative stories can motivate learning because learners:

- engage with the text and their imaginations.
- learn vocabulary with repetition of key words in the text and pictures.
- are exposed to repeated rhyme and sound patterns and accurate pronunciation.
- develop deeper social understanding by relating to characters and events in the story.
- actively engage listening skills as they predict, hypothesise and await outcomes.

Points to remember for effective learning:

- Story-reading should be interactive (teacher and learners). It should involve pointing, describing and discussing how the story relates to the real world.
- Learners will engage with a story more if they are encouraged to 'work out' the meaning, for example, why learners think characters did something or how characters felt at a certain moment and, of course, what the story 'value' is.
- Learners benefit from more than one reading or hearing of a story. At least one reading should be read/heard right the way through from beginning to end without interruption.

For more information about stories in language learning, go to

Why Cambridge English: Young Learners (YLE)?

The stories have been written to reflect the different language levels and topic areas of the Cambridge English: Starters, Movers and Flyers tests and to appeal to the target-reader age groups. The language of the stories is exploited in activities that check comprehension, teach key vocabulary and grammar, practise all four language skills (reading, writing, listening and speaking) and give learners an opportunity to familiarise themselves with the nature and format of the Cambridge English: Young Learners tests. The optional *Let's have fun!* and *Let's speak!* sections at the back of the books also provide opportunities for collaborative learning and test speaking practice. The *Let's say!* pages support early pronunciation skills, building from sounds to sentences.

There are two Student's Books for each test: pre-A1 (Starters), A1 (Movers) and A2 (Flyers). *Storyfun 3* gently introduces students to the Cambridge English: Movers language and topics through fun activities and test-style practice. Activities are carefully graded to ensure learners are guided towards the test level, with frequent opportunities to build up their language and skills. *Storyfun 4* provides full practice of all the Cambridge English: Movers test tasks. By the end of *Storyfun* levels 3 and 4, constant recycling of language and test task types ensures learners are fully prepared for the Cambridge English: Movers test.

Who is *Storyfun* for?

Storyfun has been written for teachers and young learners of English in a wide variety of situations. It is suitable for:

- learners in this age group who enjoy reading and listening to stories
- large and small groups of learners
- monolingual and multilingual classes
- learners who are beginning to prepare to take the Cambridge English: Movers test
- young learners who need to develop their vocabulary, grammar and language
- young learners keen to discuss social values, develop collaborative learning skills and build confidence for the Movers Speaking paper
- teachers who wish to develop their learners' literacy skills

What are the key features of *Storyfun 3*?

Student's Book

- eight imaginative and motivating stories
- fun, interactive, creative and meaningful activities
- activities similar to task types found in all three parts (Reading and Writing, Listening and Speaking) of the Cambridge English: Movers test

- o an introduction to Cambridge English: Movers grammar and vocabulary
- o extension activities *Let's have fun!*, further speaking practice *Let's speak!* and an early pronunciation focus *Let's say!*
- o unit-by-unit word list

Home FUN booklet

- o fun activities for learners to try at home
- o 'self-assessment' activities that build learners' confidence and encourage autonomy
- o a Cambridge English: Movers picture dictionary
- o *Let's have fun!* pages to encourage learners to use English in the wider world
- o answers, audio and additional support found online by using the code at the front of this book.

Teacher's Book with Audio

- o a map of the Student's Book (topics, grammar points and Movers test practice for each unit)
- o practical step-by-step notes with suggestions for:

  - ✓ personalisation at presentation and practice stages
  - ✓ skills work: reading, writing, listening, speaking, drawing and colouring
  - ✓ pair and group work
  - ✓ puzzles, games, poems and songs
  - ✓ speaking activities and projects
  - ✓ discussion tasks to explore the story 'value'
  - ✓ recycling of language
  - ✓ incorporating digital materials into the lesson

- o Cambridge English: Movers test tips
- o full audioscripts
- o imaginative audio recordings for stories and activities (downloadable by using the access code at the front of this book) reflective of the Cambridge English: Movers Listening test
- o photocopiable pages for the Student's Book or optional extension activities
- o links to online practice and the Home FUN booklet

Presentation plus

- o digital version of all Student's Book pages
- o interactive Student's Book activities
- o audio played directly from the digital page
- o digital flashcards with audio
- o digital slideshow of every story
- o an Image carousel that provides further visuals associated with story themes
- o integrated tools to make notes and highlight activities

Online Practice

For the Teacher
- o Presentation plus
- o All audio recordings
- o Additional digital resources to support your classes

For the Student
- o Fun activities to practise the exam, skills and language
- o All audio recordings
- o Additional digital resources

Word FUN World App

- o Cambridge English: Young Learners vocabulary game
- o For mobile phones and tablets

Storytelling

Why should we use stories in language learning classes?

There are several reasons! A good story encourages us to turn the next page and read more. We want to find out what happens next and what the main characters do and say to each other. We may feel excited, sad, afraid, angry or really happy. The experience of reading or listening to a story is likely to make us 'feel' that we are part of the story, too. Just like in our 'real' lives, we might love or hate different characters. Perhaps we recognise ourselves or other people we know in some of the story characters. Perhaps they have similar talents, ambitions, weaknesses or problems.

Because of this natural connection with story characters, our brains process the reading of stories differently from the way we read factual information. This is because our brains don't always recognise the difference between an imagined situation and a real one so the characters become 'alive' to us. What they say or do is therefore <u>much more meaningful</u>. The words and structures that relate a story's events, descriptions and conversations are processed by learners in a deeper way.

Encouraging learners to read or listen to stories should therefore help them to learn a second language in a way that is not only fun, but memorable.

How else do stories help?

Stories don't only offer the young reader a chance to learn more vocabulary and develop their grammatical skills. The experience also creates an opportunity to develop critical and creative thinking, emotional literacy and social skills. As learners read a story, they will be imagining far more details than its words communicate. Each learner will, subconsciously, be 'animating' the characters and making judgements and predictions about events.

As a teacher, you can encourage creativity and critical thinking by asking learners in groups to develop characters in more detail, talk about the part of the story they enjoyed most/least or even write different endings. You can also discuss, in English or L1 if necessary, the story 'values', in other words, what different stories teach us about how to relate to others.

Stories also offer a forum for personalised learning. No two learners will feel exactly the same about a story and an acceptance of difference can also be interesting to explore and discuss in class.

How can we encourage learners to join in and ask parents to help?

If, at first, learners lack confidence or motivation to read stories in English, help by reading the story to them without stopping so learners are just enjoying the story, stress free, and following as well as they can by looking at the pictures. During a second reading you might encourage interaction by asking questions like *Is this funny, scary or sad?* (Starters) *Was that a good idea?* (Movers) *What do you think will happen next?* (Flyers). If the class is read to in a relaxed and fun way, learners will subconsciously relate to the reading and language learning process more confidently and positively. Of course, being read to by a parent at home, too, is also simply a lovely way to share quiet and close time. To engage parents in the language learning process, you might share some of the above points with them or encourage them to search online for language learning activities to do at home with their children.

The Home FUN booklet has been specially designed for learners to use at home with parents. Activities are fun and easy to follow, requiring little instruction. The booklet aims to help learners show parents what they have learnt at school and to engage them in the learning process.

Further suggestions for storytelling

○ Involve learners in the topic and ask guessing and prediction questions in L1 if necessary. This will engage learners in the process of storytelling and motivate learning. When you pause the audio during the story, ask learners …

> ➤ about the topic and themselves
> ➤ to guess aspects of the story
> ➤ to say how they think a character feels or what they may say next

○ If you are telling the story yourself, support your learners in any way you can by adding your own dramatisation. For instance, you can read the stories with as much animation as possible and use props such as puppets or soft toys and different voices to bring the stories to life.

○ Incorporate the use of realia into the storytelling process. For example, if you are using *Storyfun 3*, in 'High Five!' you could bring in different sports equipment, and in 'Henry's holiday' you could bring different camping equipment into the classroom to use.

○ Once learners are familiar with the story they could even act out parts of the story in role plays. This will not only involve learners in the stories and add a fun element but can also help in practising and consolidating language.

Suggestions for using the story pictures

For skills practice

○ Before listening to the story, learners look at all the pictures on the story pages and discuss in small groups who or what they think the story is about and what the key events are.

○ Learners trace a picture (adding their own choice of extra details) and then follow your colouring or drawing instructions.

To encourage creative thinking

○ Groups choose two people in a picture and imagine what they are saying to each other. They then write a question with answer or a short dialogue.

○ Groups choose a background person in a picture and invent details about him/her. For example, how old they are, what they like doing, where they live, what pet they have.

○ Groups invent details that are unseen in the picture, for example, ten things in a bag, cupboard or garden.

○ Learners imagine they are 'in' the picture. What is behind / in front of / next to them? What can they feel (the sun, a cold wind …), smell (flowers, cooking …) or hear (birds, traffic …)?

To revise vocabulary and grammar

o Learners find as many things in a picture as they can which begin with a particular letter, for example, *f*.

o Learners list things in a picture that are a certain colour or in a certain place. For example, what someone is wearing or what is on the table.

o Learners choose four things they can see in a picture and list the words according to the size of the object or length of the word. Learners could also choose things according to categories such as food or animals.

o Using the pictures to revise grammar, for example *This is / These are*.

o Choose a picture in the story and ask learners in groups to say what is happening in this part of the story.

o Practise prepositions by asking learners what they can see in a picture in different places, for example, in the box, on the table or under the tree.

o Practise question forms by asking learners about different aspects of a picture, for example: *What colour is the cat? How many ducks are there? What's the boy doing?*

o On the board, write the first and last letter of four things learners can remember in a particular story picture. Learners complete the words.

o Point to objects or people in a picture and ask *This/These yes/no* questions. For example: *Is this a shoe? Are these toys? Is this a boy? Are these hats?*

o Ask *yes/no* colour and *how many* questions. For example, point to an apple and ask *Is this apple blue? Can you see four apples?*

o Show learners a story picture for 30 seconds and then ask *What's in that picture?* Write learners' answers on the board.

o Ask simple *What's the word* questions and build on known vocabulary sets. For example: *It's green. You can eat it. It's a fruit.* (a pear / an apple / a grape / a kiwi)

Suggestions for using the word list

At the back of the Student's Book, learners will find a list of important Movers words that appear in each unit.

o Play 'Which word am I?' Learners work in pairs, looking at the word list for the unit. Choose a noun and give the class clues about it until one pair guesses it. Don't make the clues too easy and focus on form first and meaning afterwards. Say, for example: *I've got four letters. The letter 'k' is in me. You can sit on me. You can ride me to school.* (bike)

o Divide the class into A and B pairs. Learner A sits facing the board. Learner B sits with his/her back to the board. Write four words (nouns or verbs are best) from the word list for the unit on the board. Learner A then draws or mimes them until their partner guesses them all and writes them correctly (with the help of Learner A who can only say *Yes, that's right!* or *No, that's wrong!*). When everyone has finished, learners change places. Write some new words on the board. Learner B in each pair mimes these words for Learner A to guess.

o Play 'Tell me more, please!' Choose a noun from the word list for the unit and write it on the board, for example: *banana*. Learners take turns to add more information about the banana. For example, Learner A says: *The banana is long.* Learner B adds: *The banana is long. It's yellow.* Learner C says: *The banana is long. It's yellow. It's a fruit.* Continue until learners can't remember previous information.

o Pairs work together to make as many words from the word list for the unit as they can, using a number of letters that you dictate to the class. Alternatively, use word tiles from board games or letter cards made by the class. These could also be used for spelling tests in pairs or groups.

o On the board, write eight words from the word list for the unit with the letters jumbled. Pairs work as fast as they can to find the words and spell them correctly.

o On the board, write eight words from the word list for the unit. Spell three or four of them incorrectly. Pairs work as fast as they can to identify the misspelt words (they shouldn't be told how many there are) and to write them down correctly.

o Play 'Make a word'. Each group chooses a word (four, five or six letters long) from the word list for the unit and creates it by forming a human sculpture, i.e. learners in each group stand in a line, using their arms or legs to create the shapes of each letter. Remember you may need two learners for some letters (e.g. *k*). When all the groups are ready, the words are guessed.

o Use the word list for the unit to play common word games such as hangman, bingo and definition games or for dictated spelling tests. A nice alternative to the traditional hangman, which learners may enjoy, is an animal with its mouth open, with 8–10 steps leading down into its mouth. (You could use a crocodile at Starters, a shark at Movers or a dinosaur at Flyers.) With each incorrect guess, the stick person falls down onto the next step, and gets eaten if they reach the animal's mouth!

For more information on Cambridge English: Young Learners, please visit. From here, you can download the handbook for teachers, which includes information about each level of the Young Learners tests. You can also find information for candidates and their parents, including links to videos of the Speaking test at each level. There are also sample test papers, as well as further games and songs and links to the Teaching Support website.

A few final classroom points

Please try to be as encouraging as possible when working through the activities. By using phrases such as *Now you! You choose! Well done! Don't worry!* you are also helping learners to feel more confident about participating fully in the class and trying hard to do their best. Make sure that everyone in your class adds to open class work, however minimally, and when mistakes are made, view them as opportunities for learning. Try not to interrupt to correct learners during open class discussion, role plays, etc. Doing so might negatively affect a child's willingness to contribute in future. It takes courage to speak out in class. Make mental notes of mistakes and then cover them at a later moment with the whole class.

Have fun!

But most of all, please remember that an hour's lesson can feel very much longer than that to a learner who feels excluded, fearful of making mistakes, unsure about what to do, unable to follow instructions or express any personal opinions. An hour's lesson will feel like five minutes if a learner is having fun, sensing their own progress and participating fully in enjoyable and meaningful activities.

How is the Student's Book organised?

Story

Four illustrated story pages using language (topics, vocabulary and grammar) needed for the Cambridge English: Movers test.

Vocabulary activity

Each unit of four-page activities opens with a vocabulary comprehension activity related to the key Cambridge English: Movers vocabulary presented in the story.

Value key phrase

A key English phrase in a speech bubble (within the story) demonstrates the story 'value'. For example, Caring for our friends ➜ "What's the matter?"

Practice for Movers activities

gently introduce learners to the style of the Cambridge English: Movers test tasks and cover the key skills, vocabulary and grammar necessary for the test. See ➜ in the Teacher's Book for identification.

Skills

All activities develop reading, writing, listening and speaking skills that are useful for the YL tests.

⭐ Value activities

encourage learners to think about the story in a social context and practise the key English phrase. The phrase aids learners to contextualise, remember and demonstrate the value of English.

♪ Songs

Open activities such as poems and songs maintain learners' motivation and interest.

✿ Let's have fun!

Optional projects or games at the back of the Student's Book to promote collaborative learning.

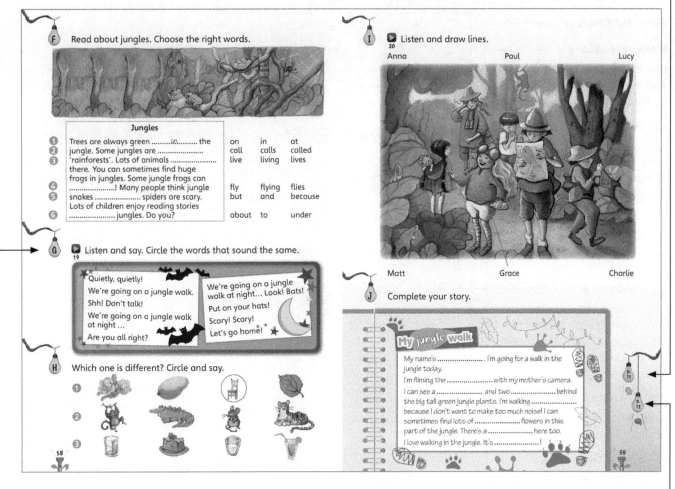

F Read about jungles. Choose the right words.

Jungles

①	Trees are always green ......in...... the	on	in	at
②	jungle. Some jungles are	call	calls	called
③	'rainforests'. Lots of animals .... there. You can sometimes find huge frogs in jungles. Some jungle frogs can	live	living	lives
④	.....................! Many people think jungle	fly	flying	flies
⑤	snakes .... spiders are scary. Lots of children enjoy reading stories	but	and	because
⑥	.... jungles. Do you?	about	to	under

G ▶ Listen and say. Circle the words that sound the same.
19

Quietly, quietly!
We're going on a jungle walk.
Shh! Don't talk!
We're going on a jungle walk at night ...
Are you all right?

We're going on a jungle walk at night... Look! Bats!
Put on your hats!
Scary! Scary!
Let's go home!

H Which one is different? Circle and say.

① ② ③

58

I ▶ Listen and draw lines.
20

Anna   Paul   Lucy

Matt   Grace   Charlie

J Complete your story.

My jungle walk

My name's .... I'm going for a walk in the jungle today.
I'm filming the .... with my mother's camera.
I can see a .... and two .... behind the big tall green jungle plants. I'm walking .... because I don't want to make too much noise! I can sometimes find lots of .... flowers in this part of the jungle. There's a .... here too.
I love walking in the jungle. It's ....!

59

▶ Accompanying audio tracks can be found on Presentation plus or online

🗨 Let's speak!

Optional extra speaking practice at the back of the Student's Book allows learners to practise the language needed for the speaking part of the Cambridge English: Movers test.

🔊 ▶ Let's say!

Optional pronunciation practice at the back of the Student's Book focuses on initial key sounds to develop early speaking skills. Supported by accompanying audio.

How could teachers use *Storyfun 3*?

1 Encourage learners to predict the general topic of the story using flashcards and the story pictures.
2 Teach or revise any Cambridge English: Movers words that are important in the story.
3 Play the audio or read the story.
4 (Optional) Discuss the story 'value' with learners. You will probably need to do this in your learners' first language to fully explore what the story teaches the reader.
5 Present the vocabulary and general comprehension tasks (usually Activities A–C).
6 Present the grammar, vocabulary and skills sections (generally Activities D–H).
7 Encourage collaborative learning with the *Let's have fun!* at the back of the Student's Book.
8 Follow communicative pair- or group-work suggestions in the *Let's speak!* pages at the back of the Student's Book.
9 Use extension activities in the Teacher's Books or set homework tasks.

How is the Teacher's Book organised?

Main topics and grammar

Cambridge English: Movers topics and grammar focused on in the activities in this unit.

Story summary

Main vocabulary

Cambridge English: Movers vocabulary focused on in the activities in this unit.

➡ Practice for Movers

Specific activities that gently build up learners' familiarity and practise for the Cambridge English: Movers test.

Equipment

Any equipment or materials needed for teaching the unit, including photocopiables, digital flashcards, audio.

Storytelling

Extended notes for approaching storytelling with your learners give detailed suggestions on how to fully exploit digital resources and prompt meaningful and motivating discussions.

☆ Value

The value can be explored and discussed with learners after reading the story. Discussion is optional, either directly after listening or when learners attempt the value activity.

Activity notes

A, B, C etc. sections correspond to Student's Book activities.

IA Interactive activity

Activity that can also be completed interactively on Presentation plus.

Extension activities

Flexible ideas to extend activities either in class or for homework.

Answer keys

Answers or suggested answers.

Test tips and practice

Specific tips for the Cambridge English: Movers test with optional accompanying activity.

▶ Audio

Track listing for accompanying audio on Presentation plus or online

Audioscripts

All scripts for listening activities in the Student's Book. Scripts for stories are not listed.

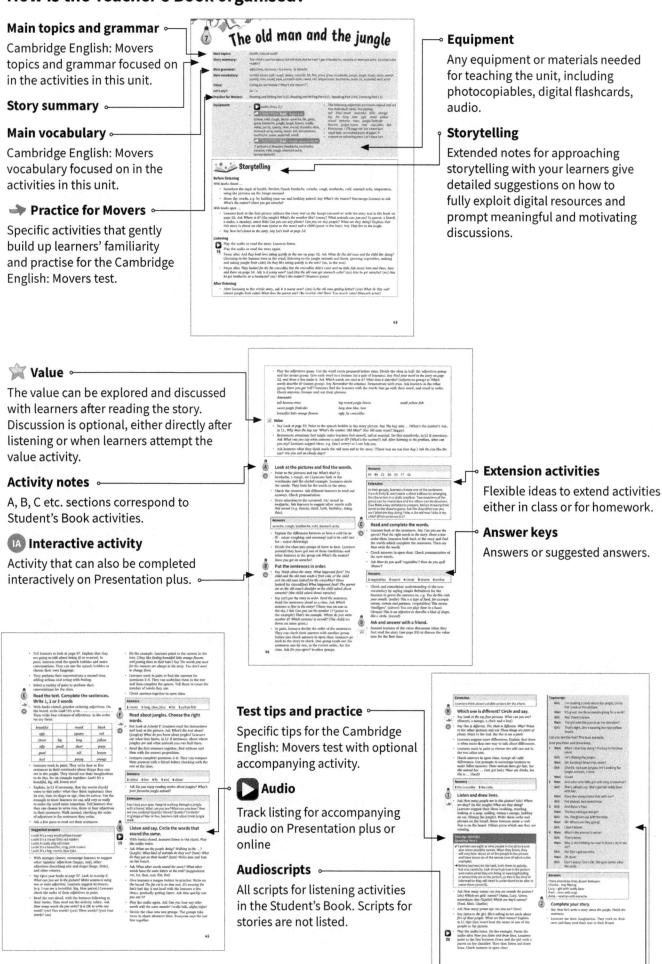

Let's have fun!

Notes for optional projects or games at the back of the Student's Book for each unit.

Let's say!

Optional pronunciation practice for each unit sections in the back of the Student's Book. *Storyfun 3* focuses on key sounds for developing speaking skills in English.

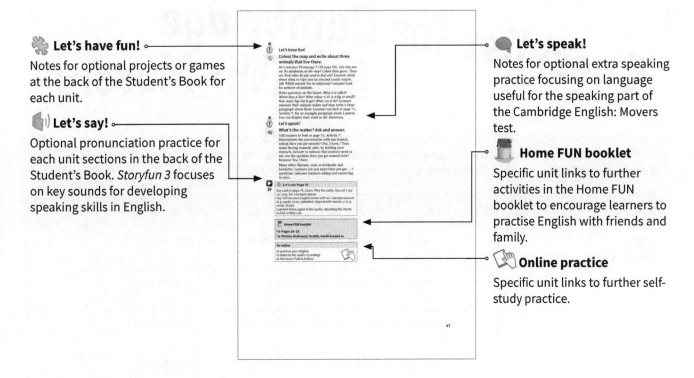

Let's speak!

Notes for optional extra speaking practice focusing on language useful for the speaking part of the Cambridge English: Movers test.

Home FUN booklet

Specific unit links to further activities in the Home FUN booklet to encourage learners to practise English with friends and family.

Online practice

Specific unit links to further self-study practice.

How is the digital organised?

Presentation plus

Interactive activities

Every 'Activity A' in each unit is interactive to check vocabulary comprehension after reading the story and encourage whole-class participation. Other IA activities can be used as a supporting feature, either as a means of introducing an activity, scaffolding, or during answer feedback.

Audio

All audio can be launched from the audio icon. Accompanying audioscripts can be displayed on screen.

Answer key

All activities have a visual answer key to easily display and check answers with your learners.

Digital flashcards

All Cambridge English: Movers test words are supported with visual flashcards with accompanying audio.

Image carousel

These additional images can be used to prompt further discussion on themes and concepts. Ideas of when and how to use them are within the teacher's notes for each unit.

Each story also has a collection of separate images of the Student's Book pictures without text to prompt discussion before learners open their books and listen, revise the story if heard in a previous lesson or to use as a wrapping-up activity where learners can re-tell the story they've listened to.

Online practice

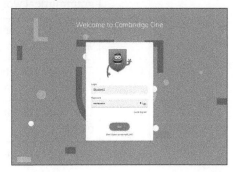

For the Teacher
- o Presentation plus
- o All audio recordings
- o Additional digital resources to support your classes

For the Student
- o Fun activities to practise the exam, skills and language
- o All audio recordings
- o Additional digital resources

Word FUN World app

Checklist for Cambridge English: Movers

Storyfun 3 gently introduces learners to Cambridge English: Movers test-style practice. Activities are carefully graded to ensure learners are guided towards the Movers level. Full examples of Cambridge English: Movers test tasks can be found in *Storyfun 4*.

Paper	Part	Task	Unit
Listening 25 minutes	1	Draw lines between names and people in a picture.	Practice: 1, 7
	2	Write words or numbers in a form.	Practice: 3, 5
	3	Match pictures with illustrated words.	Practice: 2, 4
	4	Tick boxes under the correct picture.	Practice: 8
	5	Colour different parts of a picture and write.	Practice: 3, 5
Reading and Writing 30 minutes	1	Copy correct words next to definitions.	Practice: 2, 6
	2	Choose correct response by circling a letter.	Practice: 3, 6
	3	Choose and copy missing words into a story text.	Practice: 8
	4	Complete a text by copying the correct grammatical words.	Practice: 1, 4, 7
	5	Complete sentences about a story by writing one, two or three words.	Practice: 6, 7
	6	Complete sentences, answer questions and write two sentences about a picture.	Practice: 2, 4
Speaking 5–7 minutes	1	Talk about the differences between two pictures.	Practice: 5, 8
	2	Tell a story by describing pictures.	Practice: 3, 8
	3	Say why one picture is different from three others in a set.	Practice: 1, 4, 7
	4	Answer personal questions.	Practice: 2, 6

Map of the Student's Book

Story and Unit	Value	Topics	Grammar	Practice for Movers
1 Jack and the penguins	Looking after animals (*"I'm learning a lot today!"*)	animals body food	*how much / how many* *love/enjoy* + gerund adverb (*carefully*)	Reading and Writing Part 4 Listening Part 1 Speaking Part 3
2 Jog the alien	Being kind, making friends (*"Shall I ... ?"*)	places family food	*shall* for offers *What about* + noun *like/love* + gerund	Reading and Writing Parts 1 and 6 Listening Part 3 Speaking Part 4
3 My friend Meg	Being helpful, being a good friend (*"Thanks for being my friend!"*)	friends home	conjunctions (*because*) past simple *-ed* endings *like* + gerund	Reading and Writing Part 2 Listening Parts 2 and 5 Speaking Part 2
4 High five!	Congratulating others (*"High five!"*)	sport and leisure	*can* for ability adverbs: *quickly, loudly*	Reading and Writing Parts 4 and 6 Listening Part 3 Speaking Part 3
5 The monster under my bed!	Being brave (*"I can do this!"*)	family	*have to* prepositions: *in, on, under, by* regular past tense *-ed* endings	Listening Parts 2 and 5 Speaking Part 1
6 What a great grandmother!	Trying new things (*"All right! OK!"*)	home shops	adverbs of frequency (*always, often, sometimes, never*) *after/before* + noun past simple irregular verbs	Reading and Writing Parts 1, 2 and 5 Speaking Part 4
7 The old man and the jungle	Caring for our friends (*"What's the matter?"*)	health natural world	adjectives *too much / too many* *-ly* adverbs	Reading and Writing Parts 4 and 5 Listening Part 1 Speaking Part 3
8 Henry's holiday	Finding solutions to problems (*"I know! I can ..."*)	sport and leisure	verb + infinitive (*want to*) *have (got) to* *like / doesn't like*	Reading and Writing Part 3 Listening Part 4 Speaking Parts 1 and 2

Jack and the penguins

Main topics:	animals, body, food
Story summary:	Jack goes with his dad to look after the animals at the zoo. But what food do penguins eat?
Main grammar:	*how much / how many*, *love/enjoy* + gerund, adverb (*carefully*)
Main vocabulary:	*bat, bowl, carry, cheese, dolphin, everything, feed, hungry, kangaroo, laugh, milkshake, outside, penguin, pie, sandwich, shark, smile, thirsty, wash, waterfall, zebra, zoo*
Value:	Looking after animals (*"I'm learning a lot today!"*)
Let's say!:	/s/, /z/
Practice for Movers:	Reading and Writing Part 4 (E), Speaking Part 3 (H), Listening Part 1 (I)

Equipment:

- ▶ audio: Story, I
- ➡ [presentation **PLUS**] flashcards

  Go to Presentation plus to find pictures of Movers vocabulary from Unit 1. You can use the pictures to teach/review important words in this unit.

- ➡ [presentation **PLUS**] Image carousel 1–18

  (5 pictures of animals, 2 pictures of hungry and thirsty, 10 pictures of food and drink (sandwich, milkshake, meat and potatoes, fruit, cheese, fruit juice, pie, lemonade, burger, fish), 1 picture of zoo): Storytelling, A
- pencils and crayons or colouring pencils: A, H, J, Let's have fun!
- Photocopy 1 (TB page 53): Let's have fun!

 Storytelling

Before listening

With books closed ...

- Introduce the topic. Show the photographs of animals from the Image carousel. Ask *What animals can you see?* (monkeys, dogs, cat, lion, tiger, bear) *What's this?* (a cat) *And this?* (a bear) *What's the cat on?* (a skateboard)
- Ask *Which animals do you know?* Learners say as many animals as they can. Write their suggestions on the board. Ask *What's your favourite animal? What does it look like? What does it eat?* Say to four or five learners *Tell me more about your favourite animal.*
- Review/Teach *feed* and *wash* with mime.
- Review/Teach *hungry* and *thirsty*. Show the photographs of *hungry* and *thirsty* on the Image carousel. Ask *Does he want to eat?* (yes) *Does he want to drink?* (yes)
- Look at the two story pictures without the story text on the Image carousel or with the story text in the book on page 4. Ask *Which animals can you see?* (monkey, bat, penguin, elephant, birds, giraffe, zebra, rhino, hippo, kangaroo) Say *This is Jack and this is Jack's dad, Mr Parks. What are they doing?* (learners suggest answers) Say *Jack is helping his dad at the zoo.*
- Say *Now let's listen to the story.* Say *Let's look at page 4.*

Listening

With books open ...

02

- Play the audio or read the story. Learners listen.
- Play the audio or read the story again.
- Pause after page 5. Ask *What does Jack enjoy learning about?* (animals) *Which animals can Jack feed?* (the penguins) *Where is the food for the animals?* (in the big grey cupboard in the zoo kitchen and outside)
- Pause again after page 6. Ask *Which cupboard has the food for the penguins?* (the big grey cupboard) Ask *Which cupboard does Jack look in?* (the big blue cupboard) *Do the penguins like pie and milkshake?* (no) *Do they like lemonade and sandwiches?* (no) *What do the penguins like eating?* (fish) *What do the penguins like drinking?* (water)

After listening

- Ask *What does Jack know about the animals and their food now?* (learners suggest answers, e.g. *Penguins eat fish. Penguins don't drink milkshakes. Bats don't eat burgers. Giraffes don't drink juice.*)
- Say *Jack enjoys learning about animals. Which animals do you like learning about?* In pairs, learners tell each other about their interests.

A Find and write the words.

- Ask learners *Which food words do know?* Use the Image carousel and/or other pictures to check learners' understanding of food words from the story. (sandwich, milkshake, cheese, meat, potato, pie, fruit juice, watermelon, lemonade, grape, kiwi, burger, water, fish)
- Review/Teach *plate*. Draw a plate on the board. Add a fish to the plate. Point and ask *What's this?* (a plate) *And this?* (a fish)
- Ask *Which animals are in the story?* (penguin, shark, dolphin, whale, kangaroo, bat, elephant, giraffe, zebra) Ask *Which animals live in the sea?* (shark, dolphin, whale, fish)
- Learners look at the wordsnake in Activity A. Ask *Can you see the word 'shark'?* Learners find and circle the other words. Then ask *Are they foods or sea animals?* Say *Write the food words on the plate. Write the sea animals on the shell.*
- Alternatively, learners draw the food on a plate and the animals on a shell in their notebooks.

Answers

sandwiches, milkshake and cheese on the plate; shark, dolphin and whale on the shell

B Read and answer the questions.

- Look at the example with the learners. Say *Look at page 4. Find Jack's father's name. Draw a line under it.* Learners then read questions 2–6. In pairs, they find and underline the answers in the story, and then write the answers on the lines.

Answers

2 grey **3** meat and potatoes **4** 20/twenty
5 cheese **6** elephants

- Ask learners more questions about the different foods: *Do you like drinking milkshakes? What's your favourite milkshake? Banana? Chocolate? What kind of pies do you like? Which vegetables do you enjoy eating?*

Extension

Focus on the sounds of the food and animal words. Ask *What does Jack want to give to the bats?* (burgers) *What does Jack want to give to the kangaroos?* (kiwis) *What about the giraffes?* (juice) Encourage learners to hear the repeated sounds (<u>b</u>at, <u>b</u>urger; <u>k</u>angaroo, <u>k</u>iwi; <u>g</u>iraffe, <u>j</u>uice).
Learners think about more silly foods for the zoo animals, e,g, tomatoes for the tigers. Start a funny list together on the board. Learners complete the list in pairs. Learners read out their lists. The class repeat each line, exaggerating the repeated sounds.
Write one list on the board. Learners read the list together, first quietly, then loudly, then quickly, then slowly. Divide the class into two groups. They add animal noises and actions to a final version to perform for the class. Learners decide which performance is best.

Suggested answers

Eggs for the elephants
Beans / bananas for the bats
Cakes / carrots / coconuts / coffee for the kangaroos
Peas / pears / pineapples / potatoes / pancakes / pasta for the penguins
Watermelons for the whales

C Who's talking about the story? Tick (✔) the correct box.

- Learners look at the speech bubbles and read what each child says. Ask *Which child knows our story? Is this child talking about our story too?* (no)
- Learners underline words that show differences from the story, e.g. *boy, sad*.
- In pairs, learners look at the underlined words and check their answer.

Answer

The first speech bubble is correct.

- Ask *Is it a sad story?* (no) *Is it a funny story?* (yes) Does Jack learn a lot? (yes)

D *How many?* or *How much?* Draw lines.

- Learners look at the foods in Activity D. Point to each picture and ask *What kind of food is this?* Write the learners' answers on the board.
- Draw one chip on the board. Ask *How many chips can you see?* (one) Write *1 chip*. Now draw two chips and ask again *How many chips?* (two) Write *2 chips*.
- Show learners that if we can put an 's' (or 'es' for *sandwich*) on the end of a word (1, 2, 3 chips ✓), we have to ask *How many ...?* If we can't put an 's' on the end of a word, e.g. *milk* (1, 2, 3 milks ✗), we have to ask *How much ...?*
- Look at the example together. Say *Chips has an 's'. We say 'How many chips?' Look at the line.* Learners draw lines from the foods to *How much?* or *How many?* Check the answers in open class. Learners make full questions, e.g. *How many eggs?*

Answers

How many: burgers, pears, eggs, sweets, sandwiches, pies
How much: water, cheese, rice, pasta

- In pairs, learners ask and answer questions about these food things to perform mini role plays, e.g.

How much rice do you want / would you like?	*How many sweets do you want / would you like?*
Lots, please!	*Three, please.*
Here you are.	*Here you are.*
Thanks.	*Thanks.*

E Read about bats. Choose the right words.

- Learners look at the picture. Ask *What animal is it?* (a bat) *Do you like bats? Why / Why not?* Encourage learners to tell the class what they know about bats. Mime wings. Ask *How many wings have they got?* Point to your teeth. Ask *Have they got teeth?* Ask *How many feet have they got?* Learners guess the answers they don't know.

- Say *Let's read about bats.* Look at the sentences and complete the first one together. Ask *How many words do you write?* (one) Learners complete sentences 2–6 on their own, and then check their answers in pairs. Then check answers in open class. Ask two learners to read each sentence out.

Answers

2 at **3** are **4** A **5** They **6** have

Test tip: MOVERS
Reading and Writing Part 4

✔ Learners read a factual text and choose which word (from three possible answers) should go in the grammatical gap. Only one word is correct.

→ Use three or four lines from any story text and remove key grammatical words, e.g. *because, there, to, where, are, me,* and ask learners to guess which word might fit. Accept any possible answers.

F Ask and answer the questions. Read and say.

- Talk about animals you like, e.g. *My favourite animal is a monkey. I love going to the zoo. I've got a pet dog, a pet cat and a pet bird.* Say *Ask me some questions about my favourite animal or my pets.* Write on the board *Has it got ...?* and *What colour is ...?* to help learners form questions.

- In pairs, learners read and answer the questions. Walk around and help if necessary.

- Learners tell the class about their friend. Ask, e.g. *Has (Francisco) got a pet? Would (Federica) like to go to a zoo? What's (Sofia)'s favourite animal?*

- Learners read the rhyming chant out loud. Check pronunciation. Learners make more questions with the same structure: _____s or _____s? They ask and answer in pairs. With stronger learners, ask *Why?* (because they are scary/fantastic/brilliant/dangerous/small/huge)

G How many animal words can you make? You can use the letters more than once.

- Say *Close your books, please.* Write *Jack is looking in the cupboard now* on the board. Say *Let's make animal words with these letters.* Circle the 'd', the 'o' and the 'g'. Ask *Which animal word can we make with these letters?* (dog) Learners open their books and look at the example in Activity G. Learners work in pairs. Say *Now you find animal words and write them on the lines.*

- Give learners two or three minutes to find animal words then ask *How many animal words have you got?* Ask the pair with the most words to write them on the board. Ask *Who has another word?* Add these to the board. Check spellings and pronunciation.

Suggested answers

bird, duck, goat, snake, spider, tiger, bat, bear, lion, panda, penguin, snail

- Ask *What kind of pet would you like to have?*

Extension

Ask learners to list the words from shortest to longest.

H Which one is different? Circle and say.

- Using classroom objects, explain 'odd one out'. For example, show learners a pen, a pencil, a crayon and a chair. Ask *Which one is different? Why?* (learners suggest ideas) Say *You can write with a pen, a pencil and a crayon. Can you write with a chair?* (no) *Can you sit on a chair?* (yes) Repeat using four different objects, three that are the same colour and one that is different. Ask *Which one is different? Why?* (e.g. *The table is white. The ball, the book and the crayon are green.*)

- Learners look at number 1 in Activity H. Ask *What can you see?* (a zebra, an elephant, a shark, a goat)

- Say *One is different. The shark is different.* Point to the zebra, elephant and goat and say *These animals can walk.* Point to the shark and say *But this animal can't ... (walk)*

- Learners suggest more differences, e.g. *The shark lives in the sea. The shark hasn't got any legs, but these animals have four legs.* Explain that there is often more than one way to talk about differences.

- Learners work in pairs to choose the odd one out in the three other sets.

- Check answers in open class. Accept all possible differences. Begin answers for learners to complete if necessary, e.g.
  These are girls, but this is a ... (boy)
  These are yellow but this is ... (grey)
  You can ride in these, but you can't ride in this. You ...? (wear it) *Where?* (on your head)

Answers

2 the boy
3 the grey robot
4 the baseball cap

- Revise *this* and *that, these* and *those* if necessary. Hold up your pen and say *This pen is …* (blue) Point to a pen further away and say *That pen is …* (white) Check learners' understanding. Ask *Can I touch this pen?* (yes) *Can I touch that pen?* (no) Hold up some books and say *These books are …* (new) Point to some books further away and say *Those books are …* (old) Ask *Can I touch these books?* (yes) *Can I touch those books?* (no) Point to the example speech bubbles in the book. Read them together.

Test tip: MOVERS
Speaking Part 3

✔ There is often more than one way to explain the odd one out in the set of four pictures. It doesn't matter which difference a learner talks about. The learner only needs to be able to say what is different and why.

➜ Use one set to show that different answers are possible, e.g. red shorts, grey hat, grey trousers, grey socks. An alternative answer could be *You wear these on your legs or feet, but you wear this on your head,* or *You wear trousers, socks and a hat on cold days but you wear shorts on hot days.*

Listen and draw lines.

- Learners look at the picture in Activity I. Ask *How many people are in this picture?* (six) *Where are they?* (at a zoo) *What are they doing?* (standing, sitting, walking, carrying, smiling, sitting, walking, riding animals, washing animals, feeding animals, taking photographs) Write these verbs and phrases on the board. Different learners mime a verb that is on the board. Others guess which one they are miming.

- Ask *How many names can you see outside the picture?* (six)

- Say *Listen to the girl. She's talking about five of these people. What are their names? We don't know the name of one person in the picture.*

- Play the audio twice. Do the example with the learners the first time they listen. Pause the audio after *Now you listen and draw lines.* Ask learners to point to the line between *Alex* and the boy riding the elephant. Learners then listen and draw lines from the names to the people in the picture.

03

Tapescript:

Man:	What a nice picture of the zoo!
Girl:	Yes! There's Alex.
Man:	The boy on the elephant's back?
Girl:	Yes. He loves riding that elephant. He likes washing it too!
Man:	Great!

Can you see the line? This is an example.

Now you listen and draw lines.

1	**Man:**	Who's that? The girl with the penguins.
	Girl:	Her name's Eva.
	Man:	Oh! Does she work here?
	Girl:	No, but she's helping today. She's giving the penguins their dinner!
	Man:	And they're enjoying it!

2	**Man:**	And who's that person?
	Girl:	The man with the water?
	Man:	Yes. Is that water for the animals?
	Girl:	That's right. He's called Pat. He works at this zoo.
	Man:	Right!
3	**Girl:**	And there's Sally. Can you see her?
	Man:	The girl with the camera?
	Girl:	No. The girl behind the elephant. You can't see her very well.
	Man:	Oh!
	Girl:	But she's got black hair and she's wearing a white T-shirt.
4	**Man:**	What's that boy's name?
	Girl:	The boy with the pineapple?
	Man:	Yes, that's right.
	Girl:	His name's Nick. He wants to make some pineapple juice.
	Man:	Who for?
	Girl:	I don't know! Sorry!

- Check answers in open class. Ask *What's Eva doing? What's Pat doing?* etc.

Answers

Learners draw lines:
Eva – girl feeding penguins
Pat – man carrying water
Sally – girl behind elephant
Nick – boy with pineapple

Complete your story and zoo picture.

- Say *Let's complete a story about a day at the zoo. Write one word on the lines.* Learners work in pairs and choose their own words to complete the story, and then draw a picture to illustrate it.

- Ask three or four pairs to read out their stories.

Let's have fun!

Find out more about an animal. Make a poster.

Say Choose an animal you can see on page 10. Ask *What do you know about this animal? What do you want to know?* As homework or in class, learners find out more about this kind of animal. They find information online or in books. Give each learner a copy of Photocopy 1 (TB page 53). Say *Make a poster about your animal with this. Draw or find pictures and write about your animal.* They can use Activity 1 on page 68 as a model.

In the next lesson, learners ask and answer questions about their posters in pairs.

1 *Let's speak!*

Play the game. Say more animals.

Say *Look at page 72, Activity 1*. Read the example sentences together. Ask *How do you play the game?* (you remember the animals and add one more) Demonstrate with two learners, and then play the game in open class. Learners can continue to play in smaller groups.

23

 Let's say! **Page 74**

Say *Look at page 74. Listen.* Play the audio. Say *Let's say /s/ skateboard, swim.* Learners repeat.
Say *Tell me more English words with /s/*. Learners answer (e.g. cinema, six, seven, silly). Repeat with sound /z/ (e.g. zebra, lizard).
Learners listen again to the audio, repeating the rhyme as fast as they can.

Home FUN booklet

➡ **Pages 4–5**
➡ **Picture dictionary: animals, food and drink**

Go online

to practise your English
to listen to the audio recordings
to find more FUN activities!

2

Jog the alien

Main topics:	places, family, food
Story summary:	Jog the friendly alien wants to help people. He finally meets two children who want to make friends.
Main grammar:	*shall* for offers, *What about* + noun, *like/love* + gerund
Main vocabulary:	*afraid, buy, call, car park, carry, cinema, count, cross, exciting, funfair, funny, hospital, ill, picnic, road, station, supermarket, town, town centre, vegetable*
Value:	Being kind, making friends (*"Shall I …?"*)
Let's say!:	/n/, /m/
Practice for Movers:	Reading and Writing Part 1 (E), Reading and Writing Part 6 (F), Listening Part 3 (H), Speaking Part 4 (Let's speak! / Let's have fun!)

Equipment:	
• ▶ audio: Story, E, I • **presentation PLUS** flashcards Go to Presentation plus to find pictures of Movers vocabulary from Unit 2. You can use the pictures to teach/review important words in this unit.	• ➔ **presentation PLUS** Image carousel 19–27 (9 pictures of places in town (supermarket, bookshop, car park, circus, hospital, funfair, cinema, playground, town centre)): Storytelling • crayons or colouring pens: Let's have fun! • props or costumes for reporter role play (e.g. a clipboard, a pen, sunglasses, a hat, a tablet): J (optional) • Photocopy 2 (TB page 54): Storytelling

Storytelling

Before listening

With books closed …

- Ask *What places can you see in your town?* Learners say as many places as they can. Write ideas on the board.
- Show the different places on the Image carousel and ask *What's this place? Is there a (bookshop) in your town?*
- Look at the story picture without the story text on the Image carousel or with the story text in the book on page 12. Ask *What can you see?* (learners suggest ideas) Say *This story is about an alien. Are you afraid of aliens?* (yes or no) *This alien is called Jog. He's very kind.* Check understanding of *kind.* Ask *Is he nice? Does he want to help people?* Say *Jog wants to make new friends.*
- Review/Teach *spaceship.* Draw a basic outline of a spaceship on the board and ask *What's this?*
- Say *Now let's listen to the story.* Say *Let's look at page 12.*

Listening

With books open …

 Play the audio or read the story. Learners listen.

Play the audio or read the story again.

04 Pause the audio after *Aliens LOVE counting cars* on page 13.

- Ask *What's the name of the town?* (Skiptown) *What does Jog want in the supermarket?* (vegetables) *What do aliens love eating?* (onions) *Who is in the bookshop?* (Mr and Mrs Doors) *What does Jog do in the car park?* (he eats his picnic and counts cars)
- Pause the audio again after *'No!' she says. 'But thanks for asking! Goodbye!'* at the end of page 14. Ask *Who is in the truck?* (Charlie and Lily) *Who is going to the hospital?* (Miss Kite and Miss Read) *What does Jog ask Miss Read and Miss Kite?* ('Shall I help you cross the road?' 'Shall I carry your bags for you?') *Do they say yes?* (no)
- At the end of the story, ask *What's the last place Jog went to in the town?* (the funfair) *Who does he make friends with?* (Sam and Julia) *What do they go for a ride in?* (Jog's spaceship)

After listening

- Check understanding of the story. Ask *Do Mr and Mrs Doors know that Jog is an alien?* (no) *Do Charlie and Lily know that Jog is an alien?* (no) *What about Miss Read and Miss Kite?* (no) *What about the children?* (yes)
- Give learners a copy of Photocopy 2 (TB page 54). Ask *Which characters can you see? Who is your favourite character? Which characters are clever?* (the children and Miss Kite) *Which characters are silly?* (the other adults)
- Learners read the speech bubbles and match them with the characters.

- Divide the class into groups of six. Each learner in the group chooses a different character. They talk about their character. (She's old. She's wearing a hat. She's afraid of aliens.)

 Value

- Say *Look at page 12*. Point to the thought bubble in the story picture. Say *Jog thinks ...* ('I'm not Charlie in funny clothes. I'm Jog and I'm an alien.') Do the same for pages 13 and 14.
- Ask, in L1, *Why does Jog say 'I'm not ... I'm Jog and I'm an alien'?* (the adults don't think aliens exist) Ask *Are the adults in the story kind to Jog?* (no) *Is Jog kind?* (yes) Ask for examples, in L1 if necessary (e.g. he gives the children a ride in his spaceship, he offers to help with shopping, parking, crossing the road and carrying bags).
- In L1, talk about how it is important to be kind.

A Look, read and draw lines.

- Tell learners to look at the pictures on page 16. In open class, say *Point to the circus picture. Can you see a line to the word 'circus'.* Then point to each picture in turn and ask *What's this?* (learners answer and draw lines)
- Ask *Where does Jog go first?* (to the supermarket and the car park) *Which place is opposite the supermarket?* (the bookshop) *Where does Jog count the cars?* (in the car park) *Which place is opposite the circus?* (the hospital) *Where does Jog talk to Sam and Julia?* (at the funfair) Check pronunciation and draw attention to the /s/ sound in <u>s</u>upermarket and cir<u>c</u>u<u>s</u>. Ask learners for other words they know with this sound. (centre, cinema, silly, sea, sad, Saturday)

B Put the sentences in order.

- With books closed, show learners the story pictures from the Image carousel, in a mixed order. For each picture, ask *Where is Jog? What is he doing?* Then ask *Which picture comes first? Which is next? And next?* In this way, the class create a simple spoken summary of the story together.
- Say *Open your books and look at the sentences in Activity B.* Say *Let's put the sentences in order to tell the story. What is number 1?* Learners read the example. Say *This is the first sentence of our story.* In pairs, learners read the other sentences and write the numbers in the tick boxes. Walk around, assisting as needed.

Answers

A 2 **B** 4 **C** 5 (**D** 1) **E** 3

Extension

Tell the learners, in L1 if necessary, that you are going to tell them the story again but that you are going to make some mistakes. When they hear a mistake, learners have to put up their hands and correct you. Retell the story with intentional mistakes for learners to identify, e.g.
*Jog is an alien. He's in **Hoptown** today. First he goes to the **bookshop**. He wants to buy a **tomato** for his picnic. Mr and Mrs Doors point to Jog and say 'There's a **frog** in our supermarket!'*
In small groups, learners can retell the story, adding more mistakes for their classmates to correct. Write the following structures on the board to support learners:
First he goes to ....
He wants to ....
He sees ....
He says ....
Then he goes to ....

C Answer the questions about Jog. Then answer for you.

- With books closed, ask *What do you know about Jog the alien?* (learners suggest ideas) *What does he look like? What does he like doing? What does he like eating? Do you like doing and eating the same things?*
- Learners look at Activity C and answer the questions individually. Check answers in pairs. Ask *Are your answers the same or different? Which are different? What do you love eating? What do you count? Which places in town do you go to? Which animals are you afraid of?*

Answers

1 onions **2** cars **3** cinema **4** aliens

D Draw lines and then ask and answer.

- Remind learners of the message of the story (being kind and helpful). Ask *Who is kind in the story?* (Jog)
- Ask *What kind things does Jog say?* ('Shall I get you some beans?' 'Shall I find a place for your truck here?' 'Shall I help you cross the road?' 'Shall I carry your bags?' 'Shall I take you for a ride above the town in my spaceship?') Write these questions on the board. Learners find and underline the questions in the story.
- Point to Jog's questions on the board. Say *Which question can you ask?* Mime carrying heavy bags. (learners ask you *Shall I carry your bags?*) Say *Yes, please!* and mime giving them the bag. Say *Now which question can you ask?* Mime driving a big truck and looking for a parking space. (Learners say *Shall I find a place for your truck?*) Say *No, thank you!* and continue to mime driving. Explain in L1, if necessary, that we say *Shall I ...?* or *Shall we ...?* when we would like to do something for someone. Say *It's polite to follow 'no' with 'thanks' and 'yes' with 'please'.*
- Learners look back at the story and underline *No, thanks!* and *Yes, please!*
- Do the example in Activity D in open class.
- Learners match the other offers and responses in pairs. Then they role play the scenarios in their pairs. When they finish, one pair reads out each question for the class.

Answers

2 a **3** b **4** d

E Where are the people in Mrs Doors' family? Listen and write a letter in each box.

05

- Learners look at the pictures. Ask *Where's the station? Where's the car park?* (learners point)
- Say *Mrs Doors is talking about her family. Listen.* Play the audio and pause after *Wow!* Ask *What do you write in the boxes?* (a letter) Ask *Can you see the letter B? This is the example.*
- Play the audio twice. Learners listen and write the answers.

Tapescript:

Boy:	Hello, Mrs Doors. Where's Mr Doors today?
Woman:	He's reading a book in the library.
Boy:	Oh! What's he reading about?
Woman:	Aliens.
Boy:	Wow!

Can you see the example? Now you listen and write a letter in each box.

Boy:	Where is your son?
Woman:	He is in the car park.
Boy:	Oh …
Woman:	He is washing his grandfather's car. They do that every Monday.
Boy:	And what is your brother doing now?
Woman:	Oh, he's going for his run. He does that every day.
Boy:	Where? In the park?
Woman:	Yes, that's right.
Woman:	My daughter is in town today, too.
Boy:	Where is she?
Woman:	She's at the station.
Boy:	What is she doing there?
Woman:	Having lunch with her friend. He works there.
Boy:	And where is your sister?
Woman:	Oh, she's in the cake shop.
Boy:	I love going there!
Woman:	Me too! She's buying me a cake. It's my birthday today!
Boy:	Oh! Happy birthday, Mrs Doors. Bye!

- Check answers in open class.

Answers

Mrs Doors' sister A   her son E
her brother D   her daughter C

F Look and read. Choose the correct words and write.

- Learners look at the pictures. Say *Point to the motorbike. Point to the bus. Point to the train. Point to the bookshop.* Say *You can ride on it. Which picture is it?* (a bus, a motorbike or a train) *You can buy things there.* (the town centre or a bookshop)
- Do the example together. Check that learners understand each definition is for only one picture.
- Learners read the sentences in pairs and write the

words. Check the answers in open class. Learners spell the words.

Answers

2 a motorbike   **3** a bookshop   **4** a bus
5 a playground   **6** a train

- Ask *Do you go on a train? Where do you go? Who do you go with? What do you do on a train? Do you read? Play games on your phone/tablet?*

G Look, read and write.

- Point to the picture and ask *What is this place?* (a train station) *Is the train station in your town like this? Why / Why not? What's funny in the picture? What's on top of the train?* Do number 1 as an example together: *You can see two penguins on the top of the train.*
- Learners do the activity on their own. Check answers in open class. Accept any correct answers.

Suggested answers

2 a car park / a town / a tree / the countryside
3 a green coat and a spotty dress / brown boots
4 a dog and 2/two penguins
Sample sentences for 5: It's a nice day. This is a station. The woman has got a dog. The train is blue. The penguins are funny. I can see the town.

H Look and write your shopping list. Then ask and answer.

- Divide learners into groups of four. Learners look at the picture for ideas and write a shopping list for eight different fruits or vegetables they want to buy. Encourage them to use a variety of 'crazy' numbers, e.g. *92 onions, 1 banana, 10 red grapes, melon for 22 people.*
- The group uses the list to plan a role play. Two learners are shoppers. They divide the list between them. One learner works in the fruit and vegetable shop and one is an alien.
- Write key language on the board: *Shall I …? What a kind person/alien. You're very kind.*
- Walk around and help with ideas and vocabulary. Remind learners to use *Yes, please* and *No, thanks.*

Sample role play

Shopper 1	Good morning!
Worker	Good morning!
Shopper 1	I'd like some potatoes, some mangoes, four onions and 45 grapes please.
Alien	Shall I count the grapes for you?
Shopper 1	Oh, yes, please.
Shopper 2	And I'd like some carrots, some kiwis, six bananas and 24 limes, please.
Alien	Shall I count the limes for you?
Shopper 2	No, thanks.
Worker	Shall I put them all in a bag for you?
Shopper 2	Yes, please.
Alien	Shall I carry your fruit and vegetables for you?
Shopper 1	No, thanks. Goodbye.
Alien and worker	Bye.
Shopper 2	Goodbye.
Alien and worker	Bye.

Listen and circle the correct answer. Then sing the song.

- Ask *What can people see at the circus?* (animals, clowns) *Do you like going to the circus?*

- Say *Let's listen to a song about the circus.* Say *The girl and boy are singing the song.*

06

- Point to the sentence *I'm sitting / going here with Tom and Sue.* Say *Look! There are two words. Circle the correct word.* Play the song and pause after that line. Check that learners have drawn a circle around *sitting.* Play the rest of the song. Learners listen and circle the answers. Play the song again before checking the answers in open class.

31

- You can also listen to a version of this song without the words for learners to sing along to.

Answers
sitting, Fred's, driving, silly, laughing, dancing

- Divide the class into small groups. Learners prepare actions for the song. Groups sing the song with their actions for the class. Ask *Which group has the best actions? Which group sings the loudest / the best? Which group has the most fun?* Say *Well done!* to each group for something they did well.

Read and answer the questions.

- In L1 if necessary, say *You are reporters. You want to make a TV programme about your town and what people do here.* Learners read the questions in Activity J.

- Divide the class in half. Say *You are reporters and you are shoppers.* Say *Stand up! Reporters, find a shopper! Ask the questions.* In pairs, learners ask and answer the questions. Walk around and check pronunciation. Encourage learners to mime using a microphone. They can also use a special 'reporter voice' and any other props or costumes available, e.g. a clipboard, a pen, sunglasses, a hat, a tablet. When learners have asked their questions, say *Now find another friend. Swap parts.* Learners form new pairs and play the other part.

- Ask a few pairs to perform their conversations for the class.

- Ask other pairs to report back to the class on their friend: *Does (Jorge) live in a house or a flat? How does (Yolanda) go to town? Where does (Anna) like going in her town? Which is (Paula)'s favourite shop?* etc.

Let's have fun!

Draw some shops in a street where you live. What can you buy? Write a list.

Ask *What's in the town centre in [name your town or the nearest town]? Is there a hospital? Is there a circus? What shops are there?* Say *Draw a map of your town centre. You can draw and write the names of the shops and other buildings.*

Then ask *What can you buy in the shops? Write a shopping list.*

Encourage learners to present their pictures to the class, and talk about what they can buy. Display the pictures and shopping lists as posters on the classroom walls if possible.

Let's speak!

Imagine that you're telling Jog about your town.

Go around the class pointing at each learner and saying *Alien, human, alien, human …* until each learner has been given a role. Tell the learners to form new groups of four, of only aliens and only humans.

Tell the aliens: *You are visiting [name of your town]! What questions do you want to ask? Make a list.*

Tell the humans: *You are talking to an alien about your town. What do you want to tell them? What are the best places to go?* Learners in this group can use their posters from the *Let's have fun!* section to help them.

Learners form new groups of two aliens and two humans. The humans talk about their town and then the aliens ask questions.

Test tip: MOVERS *Speaking Part 4*
✔ Learners need to be able to answer simple questions about themselves. → Make sure learners can answer simple questions about, e.g. their age, their hobbies, their likes and dislikes, their friends, their home, what they like doing at the weekend, their favourite animals/colours/ sports, how they travel to school.

24

Let's say! Page 74
Say *Look at page 74. Listen.* Play the audio. Say *Let's say /n/ in, cinema.* Learners repeat. Say *Tell me more English words with /n/.* Learners answer (e.g. nine, no, nice). Repeat with sound /m/ (e.g. mango, mum, milk). Learners listen again to the audio, repeating the rhyme as fast as they can.

Home FUN booklet
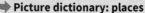 Pages 6–7 → Picture dictionary: places

Go online
to practise your English to listen to the audio recordings to find more FUN activities!

My friend Meg

3

Main topics:	friends, home
Story summary:	My friend Meg is good at lots of things, but she is always losing things. I help her find them.
Main grammar:	conjunctions (*because*), past simple *-ed* endings, *like* + gerund
Main vocabulary:	*always, board game, brilliant, bus stop, catch, classmates, comic, cool, fast, film star, homework, kitten, laptop, lose, Monday, place, pop star, sums, Sunday, table, yesterday*
Value:	Being helpful, being a good friend (*"Thanks for being my friend!"*)
Let's say!:	/r/, /l/
Practice for Movers:	Listening Part 5 (F), Reading and Writing Part 2 (G), Speaking Part 2 (H), Listening Part 2 (I)

Equipment:	
• audio: Story, F, I	• crayons or colouring pens: F, Let's speak!
• [presentation **PLUS** flashcards]	• Photocopy 3 (TB page 55): Let's have fun!
Go to Presentation plus to find pictures of Movers vocabulary from Unit 3. You can use the pictures to teach/review important words in this unit.	• the following words and phrases copied and cut into cards (enough individual cards for each learner to have three different ones): Let's speak!

cooking	riding a bike	playing tennis
drawing	spelling	climbing trees
doing homework	dancing	roller skating
finding things	making pancakes	writing funny stories

• [presentation **PLUS** Image carousel 28–31]
(pictures of trainers, pop star, film star, sum):
Storytelling, A

⭐ Storytelling

Before listening

With books closed …

• Introduce the topic of the story. Ask *Have you got a best friend? What's his/her name?* Say *This story is about a girl's best friend. Her name's Meg. Meg is always losing things.*

• Review/Teach *trainers, pop star, film star, sum* using the Image carousel. Ask *When do you wear these?* (when we do sport) *What does this person do?* (they sing / act in films) *When do you study this?* (in maths)

• Look at the pictures of Meg without the story text on the Image carousel or with the story text in the book on page 20. Ask *What's Meg like?* (She's funny. She's clever and good at riding her bike.) *How old is Meg?* (learners guess)

• Say *Now let's listen to the story.* Say *Let's look at page 20.*

Listening

With books open …

 Play the audio or read the story. Learners listen.

Play the audio or read the story again.

07

• Pause after *Go and look under your bed!* on page 21. Ask *What can't Meg find?* (her pencils) *Where does her friend tell her to look?* (under the/her bed) *Are the pencils there?* (learners guess)

• Pause again after *Go and look in your garden!* on page 22. Ask *Does Meg like wearing shoes?* (no) *What can't Meg find now?* (her trainers) *Which lesson does she need them for?* (sports) *Where does her friend tell her to look?* (garden)

• At the end of the story, ask *Has Meg got her pencils, trainers and music homework now?* (yes) *Where are Meg and her friend going now?* (to school)

After listening

• Say *Today Meg can't find her favourite pen.* Say *Let's play a game with Meg's pen. It's called 'Hide and seek'.* Explain Hide and seek in L1. Learners take turns to find a hiding place for the pen in the classroom. They write it down on the back of the paper, e.g. *Under the piano*, without their friend seeing. Then they turn the paper over. Their friend asks questions: *Is it on the chair? Is it in the cupboard? Is it behind the door?* They continue until they guess the right place. Then the learners swap roles.

⭐ Value

• Ask learners to think about the message of the story, in L1 if necessary. Ask *Are the girls good friends?* (yes) *Why does Meg say 'thank you'?* (her friend helps her find things)

• Ask *Do you help your friends? How?*

A   Read and write the words.

- Review/Teach *laptop, pop star, film star* and *kitten* using Image carousel or mime. Mime being a pop star, a kitten and working on a laptop. Ask *Who/ What am I? What am I writing on?* (a pop star, a kitten, a laptop/computer) Ask *Would you like to be a pop star or a film star? Do you have a kitten/laptop at home?*

- Learners open their books. They read the incomplete sentences and look for the missing words in the story. Do the example in open class. In pairs, learners write the missing words to complete the sentences.

- Check answers in open class. Ask different learners to read out the completed sentences. Make sure they pronounce the new words correctly.

- Write *star* on the board and underline 'st'.

- Ask *Can you say the /st/ sound?* Ask *What other words do you know with the /st/ sound?* (fanta*st*ic, ye*st*erday, *st*art, breakfa*st*, mon*st*er, *st*airs, *st*ory, etc.)

Answers

2 pop star   **3** laptop   **4** film star

B   Read and say *right* or *wrong!*

- Say something that is right and something that is wrong about your classroom, e.g. *The door is closed. Is that right?* (Yes!) *Your chairs are white. Is that right?* (No, it's wrong!)

- Say *Read the instruction.* Ask *What do you have to do?* (say *right* or *wrong*)

- Look at the example together. Ask *Is this right?* (yes) *Where does it say this in the story?* (learners point) Say *Draw a line under the answers in the story.* Learners then read sentences 2–6 and in pairs say if they are right or wrong.

- Check answers in open class.

Answers

2 Right   **3** Right   **4** Right   **5** Wrong   **6** Wrong

- Ask *Do you like drawing too? What do you like drawing? Can you play the guitar too? What can you play? How do you come to school?*

- In pairs, learners rewrite sentences 5 and 6 so that they are correct.

Suggested answers

5 Meg goes to school on a bus.
6 Meg's things are always in the wrong places.

C   When does Meg say these things? Draw lines.

- With books closed, write on the board: *pencils, comic, socks, homework, trainers, eraser.* Ask *In the story, which three things can't Meg find?* (pencils, trainers, homework)

- Learners open their books. Say *Draw a line under pencils, trainers and homework.* In pairs, learners say which lesson Meg needs each thing for. (pencils/ maths, trainers/sports, homework/music)

- They look at the line between *I can't find my pencils!* and *in the morning.* Ask *When does Meg say this?* (in the morning) Ask *Is it the morning, afternoon or evening now?* Learners draw lines connecting the other five speech bubbles to the correct time of day.

Answers

in the morning – 4
in the afternoon – 5, 6
in the evening – 2, 3

D   Draw lines. Make sentences.

- Read the first paragraph on page 20 aloud while learners follow in their books. Write on the board: *Everyone in our class likes Meg because she's always happy and she's very funny.* Ask *Why do the children in Meg's class like her?* Point to *because* and say *Because she's always happy and she's very funny!*

- Say one or two sentences about yourself with *because*, e.g. *I like (my cat) because it's (funny). We're at school today because it's (Tuesday).*

- Say *You're sitting down because ...* (we're in class / we're working) *You're all wearing shoes because ...* (we're in class / we aren't at home)

- Look at the sentences in Activity D. Do the example. Check pronunciation of *because.* Learners do the activity in pairs.

Answers

2 she enjoys drawing.   **3** she's got a sports lesson.
4 her teacher wants it.   **5** she puts things on top of it.

E   Complete the sentences with a word from the box.

- Check understanding of the verbs in the word box. Mime the words for learners to guess (played, listened, watched, painted, walked, cleaned).

- Ask *When does the girl phone Meg?* (every day) Say *Find this in the story.* Write on the board *Meg phones me or I phone her every day. It was Sunday yesterday. Meg phoned me in the morning.* Point to *phone* and *phoned* and ask learners how the meaning is different. Use L1 if necessary. Ask *When did she do it?* (Meg phones every day. She phoned yesterday.)

- Say *Look at the top of page 21. Find another word that ends in -ed.* (looked) Say *With lots of verbs, we add 'ed' or just 'd' to the end when we talk about the past.* Explain that we do this with *I, you, he, she, it, we* and *they,* e.g. *I/You/He/She/It/We/They phoned/looked.* Use L1 if necessary.

- Write on the board: *I look in my school bag every day. I looked in my sports bag ....* Ask *What word can I write here?* (yesterday)

- Learners read the example in Activity E. In pairs, learners read sentences 2–6 and look at the pictures. They decide which verb they need and complete the sentences.

F Listen and colour and write.

- Learners look at Meg's drawings on page 21. Ask questions about the colours in them, e.g. *What colour are the boy's trousers?* (green and pink)

- Learners look at the big picture on the same page. Ask *Where's Meg now?* (in her living room) *What's she doing?* (reading) *What's she reading?* (a comic)

- In pairs, learners find and write other objects in this picture (two things that begin with *a*, two things that begin with *b* and two things that begin with *c*). Write their suggestions on the board.

- Say *Now look at the same picture on page 26.* Learners look at Activity F. Ask *What's green in this picture?* (the shoe under the sofa) Say *Now colour three more things in this picture and write one word.*

- Check that learners have all their crayons.

- Say *Listen. A woman is telling a girl to colour some things in this picture.*

- Play the audio. Learners listen and colour.

08

Tapescript:

Woman:	Can you colour this picture now?
Girl:	OK. What can I colour?
Woman:	Can you see that shoe? The one under the sofa?
Girl:	Yes.
Woman:	Good. Colour it green, please.

Can you see the example? Now you listen and colour and write.

1	**Girl:**	What can I colour now?
	Woman:	Colour Meg's laptop.
	Girl:	Right! Can I colour it purple?
	Woman:	Yes, you can. Fantastic! Thanks.
2	**Girl:**	Can I write a word on the T-shirt now? The one on the floor?
	Woman:	Yes! Good idea!
	Girl:	What can I write?
	Woman:	Write her name. Write 'Meg' on it.
	Girl:	M-E-G. All right. There!

3	**Woman:**	Now colour the guitar.
	Girl:	Cool! What colour?
	Woman:	Colour it orange.
	Girl:	OK! I've got that colour.
	Woman:	Great!
4	**Woman:**	And now colour the cake. Can you see it?
	Girl:	Yes. Meg's mother is holding it.
	Woman:	That's right. Colour it pink.
	Girl:	I'm doing that now. There!
	Woman:	Very good! Thanks.

- Check the answers in open class. Ask *What's purple?* (the laptop) *What's orange?* (the guitar)

G Read the text and choose the best answer.

- Learners look at the first conversation. Say *Meg phoned her friend about her school bag. She said ...* (I can't find my school bag!) Ask *Why is there a circle around 'A'?* (it's the best answer)

- Ask two learners to role play this first conversation. They should try to use Meg and Clare's voices.

- In pairs or small groups, learners choose the best answer for the other three conversations.

- Check the answers in open class.

- Pairs role play the completed conversations.

- Ask *What are Meg's four friends called?* (Clare, Paul, Alice and Hugo) *What are your four friends called?* (Their names are ... / They're called ...)

H Look at the pictures. Write and tell the story.

- Say *Look at the pictures. They show a story. It's called 'Meg's bad day'. Look at the first picture. What can't Meg find now?* (her guitar) Say *Meg can't find her guitar.* Learners write *guitar* on the line.

- In pairs, learners look at the other pictures and write one word in the spaces to complete the sentences. Walk round and help if necessary. Pairs check their answers with another pair and make a bigger group. The groups tell the story. Ask two or three groups to tell their stories to others in the class.

Answers

guitar   car   kitchen   kitten

I Listen and write. Then write about your friend.

- Say *We know lots of things about Meg, but we don't know about her friend. Meg's friend's name is Clare.*

- Learners look at Clare's form. Ask *How many things must we find out about Clare?* (six) Say *Listen to Meg. She's telling her dad about Clare.*

- Play the audio. Learners listen and add these six pieces of information.

09

Tapescript:

Dad:	Meg, tell me about your best friend. What's her name?
Meg:	Her name's Clare, Dad.

Can you see the example? Now you listen and write.

Dad:	How old is she?
Meg:	She's nine.
Dad:	Nine?
Meg:	That's right.
Dad:	Why do you like her?
Meg:	Because she's funny. She's cool too!
Dad:	She's funny and cool?
Meg:	Yes.
Dad:	What colour is her hair?
Meg:	She's got brown hair. Her hair is brown.
Dad:	And what colour are her eyes?
Meg:	They're blue.
Dad:	Pardon? She's got blue eyes?
Meg:	Yes, that's right.
Dad:	And what does Clare like doing?
Meg:	She likes reading comics.
Dad:	I like reading comics too!
Meg:	Dad!
Dad:	Ha ha! And what sport does Clare like?
Meg:	She likes tennis. She's got a new tennis racket!
Dad:	Great!

Meg:	Clare loves working on her laptop too.
Dad:	Does she?
Meg:	Yes. She likes finding out about animals on her laptop.
Dad:	Animals? Fantastic!

- Check answers in open class.

Answers

9/nine   she's funny and cool   brown
reading comics   tennis   animals

- Say *Now you're going to write about your friend. Draw and write in the blue box.*

- Learners work on their own. Walk around and help as necessary.

- Put learners in pairs and ask *What questions do I ask to find out about your friend?* Elicit the questions and write them on the board.

- Pairs ask and answer about their friend.

3 *Let's have fun!*

What is a good friend? Do a survey. Ask your classmates.

In L1, ask about how learners choose their friends. Ask *Is it important for them to have cool clothes / mobile phones / tablets? What is important? Do they need to have the same hobbies?*

Give each learner a copy of Photocopy 3 (TB page 55). Ask *What is a good friend, for you? Look at the ideas. Tick the important ideas for you.*

Ask *Can you think about other important ideas?* Discuss in L1, e.g. the need to be kind, the need to be a good listener.

Ask *Which ideas are the most important?* Divide the class into groups to discuss.

Groups tell the class what they think. Write on the board the following structure for support: *We think good friends are ...., then ....*

Ask learners to look at the survey on Photocopy 3. First they write the full questions in the first column, e.g. *What's your favourite band?*

Then they write their answers on their own in the second column. Then ask the learners to mingle with the rest of the class, asking the questions. If they find someone with the same answer that they wrote, they should write down that person's name in the third column.

3 *Let's speak!*

Talk about things you are good at.

Say *Look at page 72, Activity 3.*

Point at the photo and ask two learners to read the conversation.

Draw a pin man on the board and say *I'm good at running/cooking/dancing. But am I good at drawing?* (no!)

Ask the class *What are you good at?* Write three or four answers on the board. Accept nouns or *-ing* forms, e.g. *football, writing stories.*

Write on the board:

Are you good at jumping?

Yes, I'm good at jumping.

No, I'm not good at jumping.

Ask three learners to come to the front of the class and role play the conversation.

Give each learner three of the cards prepared before class.

Learners read the words and phrases. Check understanding if necessary.

Point to the conversation on the board and say *Now you! Ask and answer the questions. Take your pencil.* Learners walk around and ask and answer questions. Explain, in L1, that they should tick their card each time a classmate says yes.

When learners have finished, they sit down and count the ticks.

Write on the board:

...... of my classmates are good at ....

Ask different learners to complete the sentence, e.g. **3** *of my classmates are good at* **riding a bike**. Try to cover all 12 activities in the feedback.

25

 Let's say! **Page 74**

Say *Look at page 74. Listen.* Play the audio. Say *Let's say* /r/ *really, run, race.* Learners repeat.
Say *Tell me more English words with* /r/. Learners answer (e.g. radio, read, rice). Repeat with sound /l/ (e.g. like, long).
Learners listen again to the audio, repeating the rhyme as fast as they can.

Home FUN booklet

➥ **Pages 8–9**
➥ **Picture dictionary: home**

Go online

to practise your English
to listen to the audio recordings
to find more FUN activities!

4

High five!

Main topics:	sport and leisure
Story summary:	Tom and Zoe go to a sports camp. They are surprised when they try out some new sports.
Main grammar:	*can* for ability, adverbs: *quickly, loudly*
Main vocabulary:	*band, bat, brilliant, catch, clap, dancing, fantastic, fine, ground, kick, laugh, net, practise, roller skating, skateboarding, smile, surprised, terrible, try*
Value:	Congratulating others (*"High five!"*)
Let's say!:	/b/, /v/
Practice for Movers:	Reading and Writing Part 4 (E), Listening Part 3 (F), Reading and Writing Part 6 (G), Speaking Part 3 (H)

Equipment:		
	• ▶ audio: Story, F, I	• the following phrases copied and cut into cards: Storytelling
	• 🔄 presentation **PLUS** flashcards Go to Presentation plus to find pictures of Movers vocabulary from Unit 4. You can use the pictures to teach/review important words in this unit.	*riding a bike slowly washing my face slowly eating quickly drawing quickly shouting loudly opening a box carefully climbing carefully laughing quietly waving happily throwing a ball badly driving badly*
	• 🔄 presentation **PLUS** Image carousel 32–34 (pictures of Ingrid, Joseph, table tennis): Storytelling, E	• Photocopy 4 (TB page 56): Let's have fun! • small ball, or crushed piece of paper: D • crayons or colouring pens: Let's have fun!

 Storytelling

Before listening

With books closed …

- Ask *Do you like sports? Which sports do you like? Which sports do your friends play? Which sports do you watch on TV?* As a class, use their answers to form a big spider diagram on the board of all the sports they know. Learners write the words on the board in their notebooks. Check spelling.

- Mime some of the sports for the class to guess. Ask learners to mime more sports. Make sure that the vocabulary from the story is covered (dancing, ice skating, roller skating, badminton, baseball, basketball, soccer, hockey, horse riding, skateboarding, swimming, table tennis).

- Review/Teach sports equipment. Ask *What do you need to play table tennis?* (mime hitting a ball, and point to the imaginary bat) *What do you need for skateboarding?* (a skateboard) *What do you need for soccer?* (a football, a net)

- Show learners pictures of the girl and boy from the Image carousel. Next to the pictures, or on the board, write:

Ingrid	*Joseph*
✓ *hockey*	✓ *badminton*
✗ *swimming*	✗ *table tennis*

- Say *Ingrid is good at hockey, but she isn't good at swimming. Joseph is good at badminton, but he isn't good at table tennis.* Explain that we also say *very good at* or *great at.* Ask *Which sports are you good at? Which sports are you GREAT at? Which sports are you not very good at? Which new sports do you want to try?*

- Look at the first story picture without the story text on the Image carousel or with the story text in the book on page 28. Say *This is a story about a girl called Zoe and a boy called Tom. Where are the children?* (at home) *Is Tom Zoe's cousin, brother or friend?* (learners guess) *What sports is Zoe good at? What sports is Tom good at?* (learners guess)

- Say *Now let's listen to the story.* Say *Let's look at page 28.*

Listening

With books open …

▶
10

- Play the audio or read the story. Learners listen.

- Play the audio or read the story again.

- Pause the audio at the end of the song on page 28, after *'You can do it at Treetop Park!'* Ask *What are the children listening to?* (the radio) *What can you do at Treetop Park?* (make friends, practise favourite sports and try new ones)

- Pause the audio again after *'She's fine! Don't worry!' laughs Tom* at the end of page 29. Ask *What does Zoe say? She's not good at …* (baseball) *She can't catch …* (balls) *IS she bad at baseball?* (no!) *What does she catch?* (the ball)

- Pause the audio again after *'He's fine! Don't worry!' laughs Zoe* at the end of page 30. Ask *What does Tom say? He's not good at …* (football, kicking balls) *IS he terrible at football?* (no! – he scores a goal!) *Where's the ball?* (in the net)
- After playing the rest of the story, ask *What new sports do they try?* (roller skating, basketball, skateboarding and dancing) *Do they have a good time at Treetop Park?* (yes) *Do they fall down?* (yes) *Are they OK?* (yes)

 Play the whole story again. You can also listen to a version of the *Treetop Park* song without the words for learners to sing along to.

32

After listening

- Ask, in L1 if necessary, *What do you think? Is it fun to try new things? Is it important to be good at everything?*
- Ask learners to think about all the actions in the story. Make a list, e.g. *walk, run, ride, skate, dance, play, smile, shout, throw, catch.* Ask *How many different ways can you walk?* Learners suggest ideas and demonstrate them, e.g. walking slowly, walking quickly, walking carefully, walking quietly. Write these adverbs on the board.
- Mime picking something up carefully. Ask *How am I picking this up?* (carefully) Point to *carefully* on the board.
- Use the cards prepared before class.
- Divide the class into two teams. One team comes to the front of the class; the other team watches. One learner from the first team comes to you to collect their first card and returns to their team to mime the action on the card. When a learner in a team guesses correctly, that learner comes to you for their team's second card. Continue for four minutes and then give the team a point for each action they have correctly guessed. Repeat with the other team. The team with more points is the winner.

⭐ Value

- Say *Look at page 30.* Point to the speech bubble in the story picture. Say *Zoe says …* (High five!)
- Ask, in L1, *Why does Zoe say 'High five'?* (She wants to congratulate Tom.) Accept a variety of answers, but focus on the importance of congratulating others.
- Practise *High five!* and act out scenarios in class when to say this would be good, e.g. a friend wins a race, a friend draws a fantastic picture, a friend fixed her bike.
- Ask *How does it feel when someone says 'Well done!' to you?*

A Look, read and complete the words.

- Point to the pictures in Activity A and ask questions: *What's this?* (a skateboard, a net, a band) *What's she doing?* (dancing) *What's he doing?* (roller skating) *Is he surprised?* (yes)
- Do the example. Learners do the activity. Check in open class. Check and correct pronunciation. Draw attention to the /sk/ sound in *skateboard* and *roller skating.* Ask learners to suggest other words with the same sound (e.g. score, skirt, scary, sky, skip).

Answers

2 dancing   3 surprised   4 net   5 band   6 skateboard

B Read and answer the questions.

- Write on the board:

  Question: .... ?

  Answer: Tom
- Learners suggest possible questions, e.g. *What is the name of Zoe's brother? Who scores a goal? Who hurts his leg? Who is good at soccer? Who wants to try basketball?*
- Say *Which question is in the book? Let's check. Look at the example.*
- Learners do the activity in pairs. Check answers in open class.

Answers

2 Saturday   3 Mr Hop   4 baseball   5 leg   6 soccer

- Ask *Which other day is in the story?* (Sunday) Ask *Do you know any other days of the week?* Seven learners write the days on the board. Ask *What day is it today? What day was it yesterday?*

Extension

Ask learners more questions about the story. They remain seated for 'yes' answers and stand up for 'no' answers:

Does Zoe catch the ball?	(yes)
Does Tom score a goal?	(yes)
Is the sports teacher's name Mr Jump?	(no)
Does Zoe fall and hurt her arm?	(yes)
Do Tom and Zoe try ice skating in the story?	(no)

C Look at the pictures. Tell the story.

- Ask general *What colour, Who, Where* and *What doing* questions about the pictures.
- Say *Tell a short story about these pictures.* Point to the first picture and ask *What sport is Zoe playing? Is she catching the ball?* Point to the second picture and ask *What are Tom and Zoe doing now? Are they good at this?* Point to the last picture and ask *What's Tom saying now? Are the children happy?*
- Learners then work in small groups and use their answers to tell their short story about the three pictures. They could also think of a name for their story. Walk around and help if necessary.

Suggested answer

Zoe's playing baseball. She's catching the ball. Now Zoe and Tom are roller skating. They aren't very good! But Tom says 'High five!' to his sister.

D Draw lines. Make sentences.

- With books closed, write some sentence starters on the board:

  I love playing ....

  On Saturdays I ....

  I'm good at ....

  I'm terrible at ....

- Throw a crushed piece of paper or small ball to a learner and say *I'm good at …* The learner finishes the sentence (baseball!) The learner then reads the start of another sentence, and throws the ball to another learner.

- Say *Look at page 33.* Learners read the beginnings and endings of sentences. Do the example. Learners do the activity in pairs. Check answers in open class.

Answers

2 d   **3** b   **4** c   **5** a

E Read about table tennis. Choose the right words.

- Show the class a picture of table tennis from the Image carousel. Ask *What's this?* (table tennis) *What do you need?* (a bat, a ball, a net) *How many players do you need?* (two) *Do you like table tennis? Are you good at it? Would you like to try it?*

- Do the example. Learners do the activity. Check answers in open class.

Answers

2 and   **3** their   **4** with   **5** one   **6** playing

- Ask *Do you think table tennis is an easy or difficult game? Is it good to play this inside or outside? At a school / a sports centre?*

- Tell learners in L1 that people have been playing table tennis for over a hundred years and the game started when people hit golf balls with books across a table. You can now play table tennis at the Olympic games!

Extension

Talk about a sport. Learners stop you if you make a mistake, e.g. *You need two players. You need three balls. Players kick the ball.*

F Where are Tom's sports things? Listen and write a letter in each box.

- With books closed, say *Tom is talking to his mother.* Learners look at the pictures. Say *How many different sports things can you see?* (five) *How many different places can you see?* (five) *What sports things can you see?* (a tennis racket, a baseball bat, a pair of roller skates, a skateboard, a pair of ice skates) Say *Tom's sports things are in different places. Where do you think they are?* (in the cupboard/wardrobe, under the bed) Explain that the other pictures show the places where the sports things are (in a bag, in a car, in a cupboard, in a box, in the hall). Say *Listen and write the letters.*

- Play the audio and pause after the example. Ask *Where is the tennis racket?* (in the car) *What letter is the car?* (B)

- Play the rest of the audio. Learners write the letters. Learners check in pairs and then in open class.

Tapescript:

Boy:	Hi, Mum. I can't find my new tennis racket!
Woman:	The red and grey one?
Boy:	Yes. I love playing with that one. Where is it?
Woman:	It's in Dad's car, I think. Yes, that's right. Go and get it now.

Can you see the example? Now you listen and write a letter in each box.

Boy:	And I'd like to clean my skateboard, but I can't find it.
Woman:	It's in there, Tom!
Boy:	Where, Mum?
Woman:	In the big cupboard. The one by the stairs.
Boy:	Oh! OK.
Woman:	Go and get your ice skates now, Tom. You can clean those too.
Boy:	Must I do that now?
Woman:	Yes. They're in that box.
Boy:	Which one?
Woman:	The big brown one.
Boy:	OK.
Boy:	Where are my roller skates, Mum?
Woman:	Sorry, I don't know.
Boy:	Are they in Dad's sports bag? He sometimes puts them there.
Woman:	Oh, yes. That's right.
Boy:	Thanks.
Woman:	I need your baseball bat, Tom.
Boy:	Why?
Woman:	Because I'd like to try playing baseball this evening. Where is it?
Boy:	It's by the door in the hall.
Woman:	Great! Thank you.

Answers

baseball bat E   roller skates A   skateboard C
ice skates D

G Look, read and write.

- Point to the picture and ask *Who can you see?* (Tom, Zoe, their dad) *Where are they?* (in the kitchen) *What are they wearing? What food can you see?*

- Learners do the activity on their own. In L1, remind learners they can write more than one word for answers 1–4. For 5, explain that they can choose their own sentence about the picture, so everyone might write something different and that's fine. Check answers in open class.

- Ask more questions: *Is the picture funny? Are they happy? What do you like drinking? What's your kitchen like?*

H Which one is different? Circle and say.

- Using classroom objects, demonstrate the idea of an 'odd one out'. For example, show learners a bag, a textbook, a story book and a notebook. Ask *Which one is different? Why? You can read a book, a story book and a notebook. Can you read a bag?* (no) Repeat the process with four different objects, this time choosing three objects the same colour and one which is different. Ask *Which one is different? Why?* (e.g. The pencil case is blue. The chair, book and the crayon are red.)

- Say *Look at the pictures in Activity H number 1. What can you see?* (a nose, an ear, a baseball cap, a mouth)

- Ask *Which picture is different?* Elicit *The baseball cap is different.* Point to the nose, ear and mouth and say *These are parts of your body.* Point to the baseball cap. Say *But this isn't. You wear it.*

- Learners work in pairs to choose the odd one out in the three other sets. They can talk about each odd one out in the way shown in the speech bubble.

- Check answers in open class. Accept all valid differences. Use prompts to encourage learners to make fuller answers:

  These girls are doing sports, but this girl is … (doing homework)

  These are vegetables, but this is … (a radio) or *You can eat these, but you can't eat a …* (radio) *You listen to a …* (radio)

  You hold these in your … (hand), *but you kick this with your …* (foot) or *You can hit a ball with these, but you …* (kick this)

- Review/Teach the difference between *this* and *that* and *these* and *those*.

Answers

2 girl reading **3** radio **4** football

Extension

In pairs, learners draw a set of four pictures with an 'odd one out'. Then put pairs into groups of four. One pair shows their pictures and the other pair says which picture is different and why. Walk around and check that pairs have the necessary language to talk about the odd one out. Write on the board:

[verb]
You can play these, but you can't play this. You sleep in this.
[adjective]
These are all small, but this isn't small. This is very big.
[noun]
These are all animals, but this isn't an animal. This is a tablet.

I Listen and tick (✔) the sports you hear.

- Learners look at the sports words. Describe some of the sports for learners to guess: *Which sport is it? You need a ball and a racket. This sport has two players.* (tennis) *You need a horse.* (horse riding) *You need a skateboard.* (skateboarding) *You need a big ball. You kick the ball.* (football) Encourage confident learners to suggest their own clues. Write these structures on the board for support:

  You need a ball / a racket / two players …
  You kick/hit the ball.

12

- Play the audio. Learners listen and tick the sport they hear. They can tick the boxes in any order.

- Learners listen again and check their answers. Listen a third time, pausing each time before the language comment. Ask *Can you remember what they say?* Learners call out in chorus the final comments: *Great jump! Well done! Sorry! Goal! It's really cold! Come on!*

- Check the answers in open class.

Tapescript:

1 sound of skateboarding **2** sound of ice skating
3 sound of playing tennis **4** sound of playing football
5 sound of swimming **6** sound of horse riding

Answers

The following should be ticked: ice skating, tennis, football, horse riding, swimming.

J Think of six sentences. Then mime and ask *What am I doing?*

- Write on the board: *I'm …* Mime a few verbs for the learners to guess, e.g. mime bouncing a basketball and say *I'm …* (bouncing a ball) Write the sentence on the board.

- Divide the class into small groups. Learners look at the activity. Say *Look at the verbs. Choose eight. Make sentences with them.* Learners use the verbs to make eight short and simple sentences which they write down in their groups, e.g. *I'm hitting a ball. I'm watching TV.*

- Groups take turns to mime their sentences for the rest of the class to guess the complete sentence. Alternatively, learners could just guess the verb in the sentence. Ask one person in the group to read out their sentence at the end. Write the (corrected) sentences on the board.

4 *Let's have fun!*

Make a poster and tell your classmates.

Learners think about a sport. It can be their favourite sport, or a sport they don't know well. Give a copy of Photocopy 4 (TB page 56) to each learner. They look at the ideas boxes. Ask *Can you answer the questions? What do you know about your sport? What do you want to know?* Learners find out more about the sport online or from books. They can do their research in L1 or in English. They make notes.

Say *Now let's make a poster.* Learners draw a picture of their sport, or they can cut pictures out of magazines, or print photos from the internet. They label their pictures. In small groups, learners tell their classmates about their poster.

4 *Let's speak!*

Imagine that you're making friends with Zoe.

Say *Imagine you want to make friends with Zoe. What can you say?* Brainstorm ideas from the class about what they could say to make new friends. Accept all valid answers (e.g. *I'm .... What's your name?, Hi!, Pleased to meet you.*) Say *Now look at page 72, Activity 4.* Learners look at the example speech bubbles.

In pairs, learners perform role plays. They can shake hands, or use other gestures of greeting.

Ask different pairs to perform their role play for the class.

26

| |)) *Let's say!* **Page 74**

Say *Look at page 74. Listen.* Play the audio. Say *Let's say /b/ baseball.* Learners repeat.
Say *Tell me more English words with /b/.* Learners answer (e.g. blue, burger, beach, baby). Repeat with sound /v/ (e.g. very, village, five).
Learners listen again to the audio, repeating the rhyme as fast as they can.

 Home FUN booklet

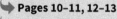 **Pages 10–11, 12–13**
Picture dictionary: sports and leisure

Go online

to practise your English
to listen to the audio recordings
to find more FUN activities!

The monster under my bed!

5

Main topics:	family
Story summary:	A girl thinks there's a monster under her bed. She's frightened and asks her family to help her, but in the end she is brave.
Main grammar:	*have to*, prepositions: *in, on, under, by*, regular past tense *-ed* endings
Main vocabulary:	*after, asleep, before, clean* (v), *downstairs, film, floor, homework, huge, parent, Saturday, scary, silly, son, stomach, sweater, teeth, uncle, upstairs, week, yesterday*
Value:	Being brave (*"I can do this!"*)
Let's say!:	/g/, /dʒ/
Practice for Movers:	Speaking Part 1 (F), Listening Part 5 (G), Listening Part 2 (J)

Equipment:

- audio: Story, G, J
- presentation **PLUS** flashcards

  Go to Presentation plus to find pictures of Movers vocabulary from Unit 5. You can use the pictures to teach/review important words in this unit.

- presentation **PLUS** Image carousel 35–41

  (pictures of monster and child, Will Smith, Rafael Nadal, David Beckham, Taylor Swift, sandwich and water, bed and phone): Storytelling, E, I
- crayons or colouring pens: G, Let's have fun!
- plain sheets of A4 paper for each learner: Let's speak!
- Photocopy 5 (TB page 57): Storytelling

 ## Storytelling

Before listening

With books closed …

- Introduce the topic of the story: *This story is about a girl. She's afraid of a monster.* Ask *Are you afraid of monsters?*
- Review/Teach *scare, hear* and *count*. Cover your ears with your hands and say *I can't hear you.* Then take your hands away and say *I can hear you now.* Use the Image carousel to teach *scare, scared* and *scary.* Count something in the classroom and then ask two or three learners *Please count the windows/desks/chairs.* They should point and say *One, two, three,* etc.
- Learners look at the first picture without the story text on the Image carousel or with the story text in the book on page 36. Ask *What kind of room is this?* (a bedroom) *Is this like your bedroom?* (learners answer) *What's the girl carrying?* (her clothes) *Why is she running?* (learners guess) Say *Now let's listen to the story.* Say *Let's look at page 36.*

Listening

With books open …

- ▶ Play the audio or read the story. Learners listen.
- **13** Play the audio or read the story again.
- Pause after *I know it's there* on page 37. Ask *What's under the girl's bed?* (a monster) *Does she enjoy playing computer games in her room?* (no) *Can the girl see the monster?* (no) *But is she afraid of the monster?* (yes)
- Pause after *I can understand that* on page 38. Ask *What does the girl do when she tries to sleep?* (counts to 100) *Who did the girl tell about the monster?* (her brother, mum, dad) *Did they help her to find the monster?* (no)

After listening

- Ask *What kind of animal is under the bed?* (learners guess) *Is it a spider?* (yes!)
- Give each learner a copy of Photocopy 5 (TB page 57).
- Read the questions together and discuss some possible answers. Learners complete the story map in pairs. Walk around, assisting as needed. A few learners present their story maps to the class.
- Ask *Did you like the story?* Learners tick the corresponding box.

☆ Value

- Ask *Is Vicky frightened of the monster at the start of the story?* (yes) *Is she frightened at the end?* (no) *Did she ask for help?* (yes) *Did someone help her?* (no) *Did she find the monster at the end?* (yes) *Was she brave?* (yes) *How does it feel when you do something brave?* (very good / scary)
- Divide the class into groups of three to four. Say *Think about a time when you might be frightened or have a friend who might be frightened.* Learners role play a scenario in which the scared person says *I'm brave. I can do this!*
- Ask *Is it good to help people who are frightened?* (yes) *Do you try to do that?* Hold a discussion in L1 if necessary.

A Read and write the words.

- Learners look at the example, then read the definitions and write the correct words in pairs.
- Check the answers in open class. Check pronunciation of the /h/ sound, and ask learners what other words they know with this sound (homework, huge, helmet, head, hop, hospital).
- Ask questions to check understanding: *What makes you laugh? What time do you get dressed in the morning? What can you climb? Where do you like hiding? When do you ask for help?*

Answers

2 get dressed   **3** climb   **4** hide   **5** help

B Read and circle the correct answer.

- Write a sentence on the board with two options, one of which is true, e.g. *There are 20 / 15 children in our class.* Ask *Which number is correct?* A learner circles the correct answer.
- Learners read the instruction. Do the example together. Ask *Where is the monster?* (in Vicky's bedroom) Say *Circle the correct word.*
- Learners complete the activity in pairs. Check answers in open class.

Answers

2 bed   **3** 100   **4** climbs   **5** pictures   **6** Vicky

- Ask *Do you count to 100 when you can't sleep?*

C Who's talking about the story? Tick (✔) the correct box.

- Say *These children are talking about two different stories. One of them read 'The monster under my bed!' and one of them read another story. Who read our story?*
- Learners read what each child says and underline words that show differences between the stories, e.g. *huge, socks, hides, bed, scary, laughed, spider, frightened, brave, room, night.*
- In pairs, learners look at the underlined words and choose their answer.
- Ask *Was it the first or second answer?*

Answer

The second speech bubble is correct.

- Ask *Why isn't it the first story?* (The monster didn't take the socks in our story.)
- Say *Which was the child's favourite picture in the story?* (The picture of the girl's room at night.)

D Complete the sentences. Write one word.

- Look at the example. Ask *How many words are in the answer?* (one) *How many words can be in each answer?* (only one)
- Review/Teach *stairs.* Draw a picture of stairs on the board and move your fingers up and down them to teach *upstairs* and *downstairs.* Ask *What's another word for 'huge'?* (big)
- Learners look at sentences 2–6, find the answers in the story and write them on the lines.
- Learners check their answers in pairs.

Answers

2 clothes   **3** computer   **4** feet   **5** homework   **6** monster

- Ask one learner to read out sentence 2. Ask *What's in a classroom cupboard / a kitchen cupboard / a cupboard in your bedroom?* Learners suggest answers, e.g. pencils / pasta / my tennis racket.

E Write *I think …* or *I know …*

- Show a photograph of someone famous using the Image carousel. Say *I know this is … I think he's 23, but I don't know.* Write the sentences on the board and underline *know* and *think.* Write *I know = This is right. I think = This is right or wrong. I don't know.*
- Ask one learner *How old are you, (Mario)?* (nine) Write on the board:

  I .... Mario is nine. Ask *Shall I write 'think' or 'know' here?* (know)

- Learners look at the example. Ask one learner to say it and then ask *Does the monster get its food from Vicky's garden at night? Yes, or 'don't know'?* (don't know)
- Learners complete sentences 2–5 on their own in pencil and then check their answers in pairs.

Suggested answers

2 I know   **3** I think   **4** I think   **5** I know

F Look at the picture on page 37. Find six differences.

- Learners look at the big picture on page 37. Ask *Where's Vicky?* (in bed) *Is she awake?* (yes)
- Learners also look at the picture in Activity F. Say *Some things in the two pictures are different. In this picture* (point to the picture on page 37) *the window is open. But in this picture* (page 41) *the window is …* (closed).
- Write this model on the board: *In this picture the window is open, but in this picture the window is closed.* Practise this in open class and leave it on the board.
- In pairs or small groups, learners find five other differences by pointing or using one or two words. They then think how to describe them in longer sentences. Walk round helping with language if necessary. Stronger learners could write the differences.
- Groups take turns to tell the class one difference.
- Check answers with the class.

Answers

In this picture there are socks on the chair, but in this picture there is a sweater on the chair.
In this picture there are no white clouds in the sky, but in this picture there are two white clouds in the sky.
In this picture we can't see Vicky's feet, but in this picture we can see Vicky's feet.
In this picture the monster is under the bed, but in this picture the monster isn't under the bed.
In this picture there are five CDs on the floor, but in this picture there are four CDs on the floor.

G Write the colours. Then look at page 38. Listen, colour and write.

- Ask the colours of a few things in the classroom. Review/Teach all the YLE colours this way (black, blue, brown, green, grey/gray, orange, pink, purple, red, white, yellow). Alternatively, ask learners to point to something that's red, blue, white, etc.
- Check spelling of all the colours. Learners label each colour in the activity.

Answers

From left to right: black, white, blue, green, brown, pink, grey/gray, orange, purple, yellow, red

- Learners look at the big picture on page 38. Ask *What can you see in this picture?* Learners put up hands to suggest answers, e.g. a boy, a bedroom, a picture, a monster, a balloon.
- Ask *Which clothes can you see in this picture?* (a dress, a T-shirt, a scarf, sweaters, trousers, shoes, socks, skates)
- Check learners have crayons. Say *Listen. A man is telling a girl to colour some things in this picture.*
- Play the audio. Learners listen and colour three more things in this picture, and write one word.

14

- Ask *What did you colour? What colour is it?*

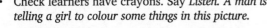

Tapescript:

Man:	Would you like to colour this picture now?
Girl:	Yes! It's Vicky's brother's bedroom, I think.
Man:	That's right. His name's Peter.
Girl:	Oh! Can I colour his scarf?
Man:	Yes! Colour it yellow.

Can you see the yellow scarf? Now you listen and colour and write.

1 **Girl:** Can I colour his roller skates now?
    Man: Yes, you can.
    Girl: Thanks. Can I colour them green?
    Man: Yes!
    Girl: Great! I'm doing that now.

2 **Girl:** What now?
    Man: Colour Peter's T-shirt.
    Girl: OK. What colour?
    Man: Colour it orange, please.
    Girl: All right. There!

3 **Man:** Now colour Peter's feet, please.
    Girl: Right! Can I colour them red?
    Man: That's a funny colour … but OK!
    Girl: Thank you.

4 **Man:** Now write another word on Vicky's balloon.
    Girl: OK. Another word under 'I'm'?
    Man Yes. Write 'brave' under 'I'm', please.
    Girl: Vicky's brave because she isn't afraid of the monster.
    Man: That's right. Fantastic! Well done!

Answers

roller skates – green   Peter's T-shirt – orange
Peter's feet – red   word on Vicky's balloon – BRAVE

- Give learners time to finish their colouring, and to show each other their pictures.

Extension

Write on the board:
Vicky's holding a ....
Peter's wearing a ....
Learners work in pairs to complete these sentences.
Suggested answers:
balloon
T-shirt and jeans

In pairs, learners then write two sentences about the picture. Walk around and help with vocabulary if necessary. Ask three or four pairs to read out their sentences.
Suggestions:
Peter is talking to Vicky.
I can see some books.
Peter's got some pictures of monsters.
Peter isn't wearing shoes.
There are lots of comics on the floor.
I can see a laptop on the table.
There are some pictures on the wall.
Peter's sweater is on the chair.
There's a rug next to Peter's bed.

H Complete the sentences with a word from the box.

- Learners look at Vicky's family tree. Explain what it is. Ask *Do you have grandparents? What are their names? Who did Vicky's dad watch TV with in the story?* (her uncle Bill) *Do you have an uncle? An aunt? What are their names?*
- Learners look at the example and then complete sentences 2–6 with the correct family word from the box. They should only write one-word answers.
- Check answers in open class.

Answers

2 parents   **3** aunt   **4** grandparents   **5** sister   **6** son

Extension

Learners draw faces and create their own family tree, adding short sentences to their picture this time, e.g. *My grandmother's name is Katia.* They could then write three or four sentences about different family members, beginning with *I think*, e.g. *I think my dad is great. I think my uncle is very nice. I think my brother is very naughty.*

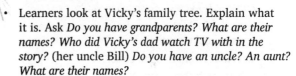

I Draw lines. Make sentences.

- Ask *In the story, what did Mum do in Vicky's room yesterday?* (she cleaned it) Ask *What does the monster do when Mum goes in Vicky's room?* (it hides)
- Write on the board: *The monster hid when Mum went in Vicky's room.*
- Show learners how *when* can join two short sentences together: *The monster hid when Mum went in my room.*
- Explain that these two things happen almost at the same time. Draw a time line to show this:

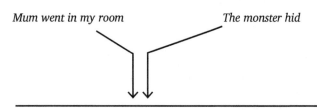

Mum went in my room   *The monster hid*

- Use the Image carousel to show a sandwich, a glass of water, a bed and a phone on the board. Point to each in turn and say *I make a sandwich when I'm hungry! I get a glass of water …* (when I'm thirsty) *I go to bed …* (when I'm tired) *I phone my friend …* (when I'm afraid)
- Write on the board: *What do you do when you're thirsty? Hungry? Tired? Sad? Afraid?* In groups of three, learners talk about what they do in these situations. Walk round and help if necessary. Prompt answers: *Do you make a sandwich when you're hungry? Do you sit down when you're tired?*
- Learners look at the example. In pairs, they draw lines to make sentences.
- Check answers in open class.

Answers

2 he got some new pencils. **3** it was my birthday.
4 they went to the beach. **5** it was dirty.

- You may like to show learners that *when* can also come at the beginning of a sentence: *When I get up in the morning, I have to run to my cupboard* (page 36).
- Write on the board: *We ………………………… when we're at school.*
- In pairs, learners complete this sentence in as many different ways as possible. Walk round and help with vocabulary if necessary.

J Listen and write about Vicky's brother.

- Learners look at the boy and the answer to number 1. Ask *Who's this?* (Peter – Vicky's brother)
- In pairs, learners look at the spaces for 2–6 and talk about Peter. Ask *What do you think the answers are?* Learners guess the answers in pairs before listening.
- Play the audio more than twice if necessary. Learners write the correct answers.

15

Answers

1 11/eleven **2** drawing **3** washing **4** blue
5 17/seventeen

- Use the picture of Peter's room on page 38 to review/teach *tidy/untidy*. Ask *Is your bedroom tidy or untidy?*

✔ Learners read five prompts, listen to a conversation that usually contains personal details and then complete a form. Sometimes, part of an answer is given before or after the gap, e.g.

Pet: a ....

Name of Jack's school: .... *School.*

→ Learners could create fact files for a classmate to complete about three or four different (imagined or real) friends, listing, e.g. *Name: Age: Pet's name: Favourite hobby: Likes eating: Is good at:* Learners take turns to ask about each friend and complete the form.

K Read the sentences and tell the story. It is called 'Don't worry!'

- Ask learners if they liked the story. Ask *What was the best part? When did you laugh?*

- Divide learners into groups of five (learners A, B, C, D and E). Write on the board: *Vicky, Mum, Grandma, Peter, Dad.*

- Groups choose their roles, plan and then practise the conversation. Each person reads out their own line, adding extra words if they like.

- When groups are ready, they take it in turns to role play the story in front of the class.

5 *Let's have fun!*

Draw and write about a monster.

Learners draw a monster and colour it. They make it scary, funny, sad, tall, short or fat.

Learners write sentences to describe their monster, e.g. *My monster lives in the kitchen. It likes eating kiwis and it's very good at jumping.* They can look at page 70, Activity 5 for a model.

5 *Let's speak!*

Draw your family tree. Tell your partner.

Give each learner a blank piece of paper. Tell learners to look at page 73, Activity 5. Explain that they are going to draw their family tree or invent a family tree. Ask who they think they should include. Tell learners they can choose. They should write the names and draw pictures or they could stick photos / print outs of scanned photos as a homework project. When learners have completed their family trees, they use them to talk about their families with a friend. Write on the board:

My grandmother's name is ....

Ask *What else can you say? What describing words do you know?* (clever, funny, tall, quiet)

Learners take turns to talk about their family tree in pairs.

  Let's say! Page 75

27 Say *Look at page 75. Listen.* Play the audio. Say *Let's say /g/ Grandma, game.* Learners repeat.
Say *Tell me more English words with /g/.* Learners answer (e.g. garden, goodbye, goat). Repeat with sound /dʒ/ (e.g. giraffe, jacket, juice).
Learners listen again to the audio, repeating the rhyme as fast as they can.

Home FUN booklet

→ Pages 14–15
→ Picture dictionary: clothes, body and face

Go online

to practise your English
to listen to the audio recordings
to find more FUN activities!

6

What a great grandmother!

Main topics:	home, shops
Story summary:	Peter's grandmother does the same things at the same time every day. One weekend, Peter and his grandmother have a crazy weekend, and do things differently!
Main grammar:	adverbs of frequency (*always, often, sometimes, never*), *after/before* + noun, past simple irregular verbs
Main vocabulary:	*after, always, around, brilliant, café, cinema, coffee, cool, cup, downstairs, every, fantastic, Friday, grandson, hungry, library, market, never, noodles, o'clock, often, pancake, ride* (n)*, river, sandwich, Saturday, sauce, shopping centre, sometimes, square, walk* (n)
Value:	Trying new things (*"All right! OK!"*)
Let's say!:	/ʃ/, /tʃ/
Practice for Movers:	Reading and Writing Part 5 (D), Reading and Writing Part 2 (G), Reading and Writing Part 1 (H), Speaking Part 4 (J)

Equipment:	
<ul><li>▶ audio: Story, K</li><li> flashcards Go to Presentation plus to find pictures of Movers vocabulary from Unit 6. You can use the pictures to teach/review important words in this unit.</li><li>presentation **PLUS** Image carousel 42–47 (6 pictures of places in town (river, café, library, cinema, market, square)): A, D</li><li>crayons or colouring pens: H, Let's have fun!</li></ul>	<ul><li>the following story sentences copied onto card and cut into sentence strips (one set for each group of four learners): Storytelling *On Saturday morning, Peter got up at seven o'clock.* *Peter and Gran had sausages for breakfast.* *They got dressed and went for a walk.* *They got a bus to Market Street.* *They walked around the shopping centre.* *For lunch, they ate noodles and pancakes in a café.* *In the afternoon, they went for a boat ride and a walk.* *Then they went to the cinema.*</li><li>Photocopy 6 (TB page 58): E</li></ul>

Storytelling

Before listening

With books closed …

- Introduce the topic of the story by saying *This story is about a boy and his grandmother. The boy's name is Peter.* Review/Teach *grandparents*. Ask *Do you have grandparents? How old are they? Do they live with your family?* Write a few answers on the board. In pairs, learners tell each other about their grandparents, if they have them, or other older people they know.
- Learners look at the first pictures without the story text on the Image carousel or with the story text in the book on page 44. Say *This is Peter's grandmother. He calls her Gran.*
- Ask *What time does she get up?* (seven o'clock) *What does she do at ten o'clock?* (she listens to the radio)
- Learners look at the other pictures and say what Peter's grandmother does at different times of the day.
- Say *Now let's listen to the story.* Say *Let's look at page 44.*

Listening

With books open …

▶ Play the audio or read the story. Learners listen.

16 Play the audio or read the story again.

- Pause after *But then she looked at Peter's face and said, 'OK!'* on page 45. Ask *Does Peter's grandmother do the same things every day?* (yes) *What does she always eat for breakfast?* (two pieces of bread, a banana and a cup of tea) *What did Peter want to have for breakfast on Saturday?* (egg sandwiches or sausages)
- Pause after *'What a great day!'* on page 46. Ask *Where did Peter and his grandmother go that morning?* (to Market Street) *Did they have fish, chips and peas for lunch?* (no – they had noodles and pancakes) *What do they do after lunch?* (learners guess)
- At the end of the story, ask *What do they do after lunch?* (They go on a boat ride and then walk around the lake. Then they go to the cinema.)

After listening

- Use the story sentence strips prepared before the lesson.

- Divide the class into groups of four. Give them a set of sentences. Say *Think about Peter and his grandmother's day. What did they do? Put the sentences in order.* Learners order the sentences from memory and then check the answers in the story.
- Collect the sets of sentences in. Give each of eight learners one sentence from a set. The learners arrange themselves in the correct order. Then they say their sentence aloud, one by one, and the rest of the class decide if the order is correct.
- Ask *What did Peter and his grandmother say at the end of the story?* ('You really are a great grandmother!' 'You really are a great grandson!')
- Tell learners to look at page 47 if they can't remember these sentences. Check understanding.

⭐ Value

- Look at Grandmother's speech bubble on page 48: *'Trying new things is fun!'*
- Ask in L1 *Which things do you do every day? Is it fun or difficult to get up at four o'clock in the morning? What about going to bed at midnight? How does it feel to try new things?*
- Divide the class into groups of four. Learners work in groups to conduct a survey. Write these three questions on the board:

  What new foods would you like to try?

  Which new places would you like to go to?

  Which new sports would you like to try?
- Learners ask the questions to everyone in their group, and write down the answers. After five minutes, ask for feedback. Learners could come to the board to add their group's answers.
- Groups plan mini role plays to perform in class. Write some structures on the board:

  Learner A: What can we do now?

  Learner B: Let's go to (choose a place)! Let's try (choose a sport)!

  Learner C: All right! / OK!

  Learner D: Cool!

A Look, read and write the word.

- Use the visuals on the Image carousel to review/teach *river, café, library, cinema, market*. Check understanding: *What's in a river?* (water, fish) *Is there a river near here? What can you do in a café?* (eat, drink) *What's in a library?* (books) *Is it a shop?* (no) *What can you see at a cinema?* (films) *What can you buy at a market?* (fruit, vegetables)
- Learners open their books and read the example. They look at the other sentences and write one word to match each definition. They can look for the words in the story.
- Ask some learners to read out the four answers. Make sure they pronounce the new words correctly. Draw attention to the /r/ sound (*river, ride*). Ask *What other words do you know which start with that sound?* (ride, roller skating, rain, radio, read, etc.)

Answers

2 café   **3** library   **4** cinema   **5** market

B Read and answer the questions.

- In pairs, learners read the questions. They find the answers in the story and underline them. Then they write the answers. Check answers in open class.
- Ask more questions: *How old are you? How old are your grandparents? Do you listen to music on the radio? What do you do on Saturdays?*

Answers

2 seven/7 o'clock   **3** (music on the) radio   **4** Saturday
5 in the park

C What did Gran eat? How did she travel? Where did she go? Circle the words.

- Ask *Did Gran eat sausages in the story?* (yes) *Did she eat burgers?* (no) Show learners that *sausages* has a circle around it. Ask *What other things did Grandmother eat? How did she travel? Where did she go? Circle the words.*
- Learners circle the words on their own. They check their answers in pairs.

Answers

The following words should be circled: noodles, sausages, pancakes, bus, boat, cinema, shopping centre, café

D Complete the sentences. Write 1, 2 or 3 words.

- Look at the example. Ask *How many words are in the answer?* (one) *How many words can be in each answer?* (one, two or three)
- Review/Teach *square*. Show learners the picture of a town square from the Image carousel. Ask *Is there a town square in your town?*
- Learners look at sentences 2–6. In pairs, learners find the answers on page 44 and write them on the lines.

Answers

2 eight/8   **3** Peter's grandmother/Gran
4 cup of coffee   **5** square   **6** chips and peas

- Ask *What do you have for lunch? Do you always have the same thing? Where do you eat lunch? Who do you eat lunch with?*
- Write these questions on the board. Learners ask and answer the questions in pairs.
- Ask different pairs to say the answer to one question, e.g. *(Luis), what does (Paola) have for lunch?*

E Circle *always, often, sometimes* and *never* in these sentences.

- Learners read the four sentences from the story and circle *always, often, sometimes* and *never*.

Complete the sentences with *always, often, sometimes* or *never*.

- Learners tell you the school days of the week. Write these in a line on the board. Say *We start lessons at (nine o'clock) on Monday, Tuesday, Wednesday, Thursday and Friday.* Tick each day. Say *We always start lessons at (nine o'clock).* Use other sentences with *often, sometimes* and *never*, e.g. *We often learn new English words. I sometimes give you homework. You never have lessons in the evening.*

	Monday	Tuesday	Wednesday	Thursday	Friday
always	✓	✓	✓	✓	✓
often	✓	✓	✓	✓	
sometimes		✓			✓
never					

- Say *Tell me something that Peter's grandmother always does in the mornings.* (gets up at seven o'clock) *What does she never do?* (has sausages for breakfast)
- In pairs, learners look at pages 44–45 and tell each other more things that Gran always/never does.
- Say *I often go for a walk in the morning. Do you? I sometimes go for a run in the park. Do you?* Learners answer. Learners now look at the four sentences in the activity and complete them. Walk round and help if necessary. Pairs compare their answers. Ask *Which answers are the same? Which are different?* In open class, ask one or two learners about their sentences.
- Divide the class into groups of four or five. Give each group a copy of Photocopy 6 (TB page 58).
- All the learners in the group write their names at the top and then each learner puts a tick in one of the boxes next to the first three sentences. Everyone in the group answers these three questions before they move on to the next set of sentences.

- When groups have finished, ask them to comment on a few of their survey answers, e.g. *All of us always go to bed before eleven o'clock.* (Teresa) *and I often walk to school.* (Mario) *sometimes reads in the bath.*
- You could display the finished surveys around the classroom.

F Look at the picture on page 45. Find six differences.

- Learners look at the picture on page 45. Ask *Where are Peter and his grandmother?* (in the kitchen) *Is it the morning or the afternoon?* (the morning)
- Learners also look at the picture in Activity F. Say *Some things in the two pictures are different. In this picture* (point to the picture on page 45) *it's sunny outside. But in this picture* (page 49) *it is ...* (snowing outside)
- Write the model on the board:

  In this picture it is sunny outside, but in this picture it is snowing outside.

  Practise this in open class and leave it on the board.

- In pairs or small groups, learners point to five other differences or just use key words to express the differences, e.g. *seven o'clock, nine o'clock.* They then think how to describe the differences in full sentences.
- When checking answers, groups take turns to say one difference each.

G Read the text and choose the best answer.

- Learners look at the first conversation. Say *What does Peter want for breakfast? What does he say?* (Let's have sausages!) *Which is the best answer? A, B or C?* (A) Learners look at the circle around the letter A. Two learners role play the conversation using Peter's voice and Gran's voice.
- In pairs or small groups, learners choose the best answer for the other three conversations.
- Check the answers.

- Review/Teach *before* and *after* + noun. Write on the board: *8 o'clock: gets dressed, 9 o'clock: has breakfast, 10 o'clock: listens to the radio.* Say *Grandmother has breakfast at nine o'clock. She gets dressed at eight – before breakfast. She listens to the radio at ten – after breakfast.*
- Ask *What do you do before breakfast? What do you do after breakfast?* Learners answer.
- In pairs, learners ask and answer: *What do you do before/after dinner/school?*

H Read and write the words.

- Ask learners to look at the crossword. Read the first clue together. Ask *What does Grandmother eat for breakfast with Peter?* (sausages) *Can you see the word? Sausages is the answer for number 1.* Ask *Which word can you see at the top?* (sausages)
- Say *Now you read the other sentences and write the food words.* In pairs, learners read the clues and complete the crossword. Say *Now add two letters and make the number 10 word. What is it?* (grandmother)

I Choose new words for the green words. Write a different story!

- Learners look at the text. Say *This is the end of the story. You can change the green words now.* Do the example together. Ask *Where can you go for a boat ride?* (learners suggest ideas) Show the class that in the text Peter and his grandmother go for a boat ride on the river. In the example, this is changed to a boat ride at the beach.
- In pairs, learners then replace the green words. They choose new words, writing more than one word in each space if they like.
- Pairs read their new story to the class.

- Learners choose a new name for the story. Ask for three ideas, e.g. *A crazy day, Grandmother has a pizza, Peter's day in town.* Write the new names on the board. Learners vote for their favourite name.

J Complete the text about your day in town.

- Look at the first incomplete sentence with the class. Ask *What shall we put here? You choose!* Accept any answers that make sense for the two spaces, e.g. *school, lunch, uncle, grandpa, two best friends.* Learners write their own choices on the lines.
- Divide the class into small groups so learners can exchange ideas and help each other to plan a day in town. Each learner then completes the sentences on their own. Check answers.

K How did Gran go to each place? Listen and write a letter in each box.

- For each picture, ask *What's Grandmother doing? Do your grandparents do these things?* Ask *What is she wearing in the first picture? Where is she wearing white trousers / a yellow dress / a pink hat? Where is she NOT wearing her glasses?*
- Ask *Where is she sitting down? Where is she standing up? Where is she waving? Holding a racket? Having a sandwich? Having a ride? In some water?*
- Learners look at the transport pictures. They say the name of each type of transport (car, bike, bus, motorbike, lorry, train).
- Say *Gran phoned Peter to tell him about her busy week. Which transport did she use for each activity?*
- **17** Play the audio, pausing after *I had a picnic there. It was good fun.* Ask the class which letter is beside the park picture (C). Learners then listen to the rest of the audio and write the letter next to the correct picture on their own.

Tapescript:	
Boy:	Hi, Gran. How are you?
Woman:	Oh, hello, Peter. I'm fine thanks. I went to the park today.
Boy:	Oh! On the bus?
Woman:	Yes. I had a picnic there. It was good fun.
Can you see the example? Now you listen and write a letter in each box.	
Woman:	I went to the zoo, too, last weekend.
Boy:	Did you go there on your motorbike?
Woman:	No, I went in my car. I love going there. I had a ride on an elephant!
Boy:	Wow!
Boy:	What about yesterday?
Woman:	Oh! That was a brilliant day. I played tennis with a friend.
Boy:	Really?
Woman:	Yes! I went on the train. It's great because it stops next to the sports centre.
Woman:	And I went fishing one day.
Boy:	At the beach?
Woman:	Yes. On the rocks there. I went with Mr Jim.
Boy:	With Mr Jim?
Woman:	Yes! The seats in his lorry are really nice.

Boy:	I want to go for a walk by the river again.
Woman:	Oh! I went there on Thursday.
Boy:	On your bike?
Woman:	Yes. I went swimming there, too, but the water was very cold!
Boy:	You're very brave, Gran.
Woman:	I know! Ha ha.

- Check answers by asking *Which place matches A?* (the zoo) *Which place matches B?* (the river), etc.

Answers
sports centre F   beach E   zoo A   river B

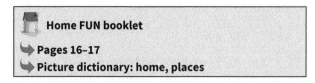

Home FUN booklet

Pages 16–17
Picture dictionary: home, places

Go online

to practise your English
to listen to the audio recordings
to find more FUN activities!

6 *Let's have fun!*

Draw and write about someone funny in your family.

Give each learner a piece of blank paper for a poster. Say *Now you draw and write about a funny person in your family. Think! What's his or her name? How old is he or she? What does he or she like doing?* Encourage learners to suggest a range of crazy answers. Tell them to be imaginative. They can think about silly ideas (it doesn't have to be a real person).

They copy and complete the sentences from page 70, Activity 6 and then they draw a picture.

Display the posters on the classroom walls if possible.

6 *Let's speak!*

Talk about your day. Ask and answer.

Tell learners to look at page 73, Activity 6. Say *Talk about your day. Ask and answer.* Encourage learners to practise by asking you some questions, and answer them.

Learners take turns asking their partner questions and giving answers.

Learners report back to the class, giving one piece of wrong information for the class to identify. Demonstrate with one learner.

Give learners a few minutes to plan their answers in pairs. Suggest other crazy ideas such as funny pets (bats, monkeys, monsters) or activities. (Before breakfast she eats ice cream / she cooks banana soup.)

28

🔊 *Let's say!* **Page 75**
Say *Look at page 75. Listen.* Play the audio. Say *Let's say /ʃ/ milkshake, shopping.* Learners repeat. Say *Tell me more English words with /ʃ/.* Learners answer (e.g. shoe, short, shell, shirt). Repeat with sound /tʃ/ (e.g. chips, chocolate). Learners listen again to the audio, repeating the rhyme as fast as they can.

The old man and the jungle

7

Main topics:	health, natural world
Story summary:	The child is worried about the old man, but he hasn't got a headache, earache or stomach-ache. So what's the matter?
Main grammar:	adjectives, *too much / too many*, *-ly* adverbs
Main vocabulary:	*careful, clever, cold, cough, dance, earache, fat, fine, grass, grow, headache, jungle, laugh, loudly, noise, parrot, quietly, river, round, slow, stomach-ache, sweet, tall, temperature, toothache, water* (v)*, waterfall, well, wind*
Value:	Caring for our friends (*"What's the matter?"*)
Let's say!:	/æ/, /ʌ/
Practice for Movers:	Reading and Writing Part 5 (E), Reading and Writing Part 4 (F), Speaking Part 3 (H), Listening Part 1 (I)

Equipment:	• audio: Story, G, I • (presentation **PLUS**) flashcards Go to Presentation plus to find pictures of Movers vocabulary from Unit 7. You can use the pictures to teach/review important words in this unit. • (presentation **PLUS**) Image carousel 48–54 (7 pictures of illnesses (headache, toothache, earache, cold, cough, stomach-ache, temperatature)): Storytelling	• the following adjectives and nouns copied and cut into individual cards: Storytelling *tall blue sweet beautiful little orange big fat long slow ugly small yellow round banana trees jungle fruit cake flowers jungle leaves river crocodiles fish* • Photocopy 7 (TB page 59): Let's have fun! • small ball, or crushed piece of paper: F • crayons or colouring pens: Let's have fun!

★ Storytelling

Before listening

With books closed …

- Introduce the topic of health. Review/Teach *headache, earache, cough, toothache, cold, stomach-ache, temperature,* using the pictures on the Image carousel.
- Mime the words, e.g. by holding your ear and looking pained. Say *What's the matter with me?* Encourage learners to ask *What's the matter? Have you got earache?*
- Learners look at the first picture without the story text on the Image carousel or with the story text in the book on page 52. Ask *What is this place?* (the jungle) *What's the weather like?* (sunny) *What animals can you see?* (a parrot, a lizard, a snake, a monkey, some fish) *Can you see any plants? Can you see any people? What are they doing?* Explain that this story is about an old man (point to the man) and a child (point to the boy). Say *They live in the jungle.*
- Say *Now let's listen to the story.* Say *Let's look at page 52.*

Listening

With books open …

Play the audio or read the story. Learners listen.

18 Play the audio or read the story again.

- Pause after *And they both love sitting quietly in the sun* on page 52. Ask *What do the old man and the child like doing?* (listening to the banana trees in the wind, listening to the jungle animals and birds, growing vegetables, making and eating jungle fruit cake) *Do they like sitting quietly in the rain?* (no, in the sun)
- Pause after *They looked for the fat crocodiles but the crocodiles didn't come and no little fish swam here and there, here and there* on page 54. Ask *Is it sunny now?* (no) *Has the old man got stomach-ache?* (no) *Has he got earache?* (no) *Has he got toothache or a headache?* (no) *What's the matter?* (learners guess)

After listening

- After listening to the whole story, ask *Is it sunny now?* (yes) *Is the old man getting better?* (yes) *What do they eat?* (sweet jungle fruit cake) *What does the parrot say?* (Be careful, Old Man! Too much cake! Stomach-ache!)

- Play the adjectives game. Use the word cards prepared before class. Divide the class in half: the adjectives group and the nouns group. Give each word to a learner (or a pair of learners). Say *Find your word in the story on page 52, and draw a line under it.* Ask *Which words are next to it? What does it describe?* (adjectives group) or *Which words describe it?* (nouns group). Say *Remember the sentence.* Demonstrate with *trees.* Ask learners in the other group *Have you got 'tall'?* Learners find the learners with the words that go with their word, and stand in order. Check answers. Groups read out their phrases.

Answers:

tall banana trees   *big round jungle leaves*   *small yellow fish*

sweet jungle fruit cake   *long slow blue river*

beautiful little orange flowers   *ugly fat crocodiles*

⭐ Value

- Say *Look at page 53.* Point to the speech bubble in the story picture. Say *The boy asks ...* (What's the matter?) Ask, in L1, *Why does the boy say 'What's the matter, Old Man?'* (the old man wasn't happy)
- Brainstorm situations that might make learners feel unwell, sad or worried. Do this sensitively, in L1 if necessary. Ask *What can you say when someone is sad or ill?* (What's the matter?) Ask *After listening to the problem, what can you say?* Learners suggest ideas, e.g. *Don't worry!* or *I can help you.*
- Ask learners what they think made the old man sad in the story. (There was no sun that day.) Ask *Do you like the sun? Are you sad on cloudy days?*

A Look at the pictures and find the words.

- Point to the pictures and say *What's this?* (a headache, a cough, etc.) Learners look at the wordsnake and the circled example. Learners circle the words. They look for the words in the story.
- Check the answers. Ask different learners to read out answers. Check pronunciation.
- Draw attention to the unvoiced /θ/ sound in *toothache.* Ask learners to suggest other words with this sound (e.g. thanks, think, bath, birthday, thing, thin).

Answers

earache, cough, toothache, cold, stomach-ache

- Explain the difference between *to have a cold* (to be ill – mime coughing and sneezing) and *to be cold* (not hot – mime shivering).
- Divide the class into groups of three to four. Learners mime having a cough/cold, etc., and other learners in the group ask *What's the matter? Have you got an earache?*

B Put the sentences in order.

- Say *Think about the story. What happened first? The child and the old man made a fruit cake or the child and the old man looked for the crocodiles?* (they looked for crocodiles) *What happened first? The parrot sat on the old man's shoulder or the child asked about earache?* (the child asked about earache)
- Say *Let's put the story in order. Read the sentences.* Read the sentences aloud as a class. Ask *Which sentence is first in the story?* (There was no sun in the sky.) Ask *Can you see the number 1?* (point to the example) *That's the example. Where do you write number 2? Which sentence is second?* (The child sat down on some grass.)
- In pairs, learners decide the order of the sentences. They can check their answers with another group before you check answers in open class. Learners go back to the story to check. One group reads out the sentences one by one, in the correct order, for the class. Ask *Do you agree?* to other groups.

Answers

A4	B6	C1	D5	E3	F7	G2

Extension

In their groups, learners choose one of the sentences from Activity B, and recreate the scene by pretending to be the character(s). They can stand or sit but cannot move or talk. Two members of the group can be characters and the others can be directors. Give them a few minutes to prepare, before showing their scene to the class to guess. Ask the class *What can you see? What are they doing? Who is the old man? Who is the child? Which sentence is it?*

C Read and complete the words.

- Learners look at the sentences. Say *Can you see the spaces? Find the right words in the story. Draw a line under them.* Learners look back at the story and find the words which complete the sentences. Then say *Now write the words.*
- Check answers in open class. Check pronunciation of the new words.
- Ask *How do you spell 'vegetables'? How do you spell 'drums'?*

Answers

2 vegetables	**3** round	**4** clever	**5** drums	**6** smiles

- Check and consolidate understanding of the new vocabulary by saying simple definitions for the learners to guess the answers to, e.g. *You do this with your mouth.* (smile) *This is a type of food, for example onions, carrots and potatoes.* (vegetables) *This means 'intelligent'.* (clever) *You can play these in a band.* (drums) *This is an adjective to describe a kind of shape, like a circle.* (round)

D Ask and answer with a friend.

- Remind learners of the value discussion when they first read the story (see page 53) or discuss the value now for the first time.

- Tell learners to look at page 57. Explain, in L1 if necessary, that they are going to talk about being ill or worried. In pairs, learners read the speech bubbles and make conversations. They can use the speech bubbles or choose their own language.
- They role play their conversations a second time, adding actions and acting with feeling.
- Different pairs role play their conversations for the class.

E Read the text. Complete the sentences. Write 1, 2 or 3 words.

- With books closed, practise ordering adjectives. On the board, write *Look! It's a/an* .... Then write four columns of adjectives, in the order we say them:

beautiful		round	black
ugly		square	red
clever	big	long	yellow
silly	small	short	green
good		old	brown
bad		young	orange

- Learners work in pairs. They write four or five sentences in their notebooks about things they can see in the jungle. They should use their imaginations to do this. Do an example together: *Look! It's a beautiful, big, old, brown tree!*
- Explain, in L1 if necessary, that the words should come in this order: what they think (opinions), then its size, then its shape or age, then its colour. Use the example to show learners we can add *very* or *really* to make the word more important. Tell learners that they can choose to write two, three or four adjectives in their sentences. Walk around, checking the order of adjectives in the sentences they write.
- Ask a few pairs to read out their sentences.

Suggested answers

Look! It's a very ugly yellow house!
Look! It's a clever red spider!
Look! It's a really silly old man!
Look! It's a beautiful, long, red snake!
Look! It's a big, round, green lake.

- With stronger classes, encourage learners to suggest other 'opinion' adjectives (happy, sad), other adjectives describing size and shape (huge, little), and other colours.
- Say *Open your books at page 57. Look at Activity E. What can you see in the picture? Make sentences using two or more adjectives.* Learners suggest sentences. (E.g. *I can see a beautiful, big, blue parrot.*) Learners check the order of their adjectives in pairs.
- Read the text aloud, with the learners following in their books. Then read out the instruction. Ask *How many words do you write? Is it OK to write one word?* (yes) *Two words?* (yes) *Three words?* (yes) *Four words?* (no)

- Do the example. Learners point to the answer in the text. (*They like finding beautiful little orange flowers and putting them in their hair.*) Say *The words you need for the answers are always in the story. You don't need to change them.*
- Learners work in pairs to find the answers for questions 2–5. They can underline them in the text and then complete the spaces. Tell them to count the number of words they use.
- Check answers together in open class.

Answers

2 round **3** long, slow, blue **4** fat **5** yellow fish

F Read about jungles. Choose the right words.

- Say *Look at Activity F.* Learners read the instructions and look at the picture. Ask *What's the text about?* (jungles) *What do you know about jungles?* Learners say what they know, in L1 if necessary, about where jungles are and what animals you can find there.
- Read the first sentence together, first without and then with the correct preposition.
- Learners complete questions 2–6. They can compare their answers with a friend before checking with the rest of the class.

Answers

2 called **3** live **4** fly **5** and **6** about

- Ask *Do you enjoy reading stories about jungles? What's your favourite jungle animal?*

Extension

Say *Close your eyes. Imagine walking through a jungle with a friend. What can you see? What can you hear? How are you walking? Quickly? Slowly? Quietly? Carefully?* In groups of four or five, learners talk about their jungle walk.

G Listen and say. Circle the words that sound the same.

19

- With books closed, learners listen to the chant. Play the audio twice.
- Ask *What are the people doing? Walking in the …?* (jungle) *What kind of animals do they see?* (bats) *What do they put on their heads?* (hats) Write *bats* and *hats* on the board.
- Ask *What other words sound the same? What other words have the same letters at the end?* (suggestions: cat, fat, that, mat, flat, Pat)
- Give learners a tongue twister to practise. Write on the board *The fat cat is on that mat. It's wearing the bat's hat!* Say it out loud with the learners a few times, gradually getting faster. Ask *How quickly can you say it?*
- Play the audio again. Ask *Can you hear any other words with the same end sounds?* (walk/talk, night/right)
- Divide the class into two groups. The groups take turns to chant alternate lines. Everyone says the last line together.

<table>
<tr><td colspan="2">

</td></tr>
</table>

Extension	**Tapescript:**

Extension

Learners think about suitable actions for the chant.

H Which one is different? Circle and say.

- Say *Look at the top four pictures. What can you see?* (flowers, a mango, a chair and a leaf)

- Say *One is different. The chair is different. Why?* Point to the other pictures and say *These things are parts of plants.* Point to the chair. *But this is not a plant.*

- Learners suggest more differences. Explain that there is often more than one way to talk about differences.

- Learners work in pairs to choose the odd one out in the two other sets.

- Check answers in open class. Accept all valid differences. Use prompts to encourage learners to make fuller answers: *These animals have got hair, but this animal has ...* (not got hair) *These are drinks, but this is ...* (food)

Answers

2 the crocodile **3** the cake

I Listen and draw lines.

- Ask *How many people are in this picture?* (six) *Where are they?* (in the jungle) *What are they doing?* Learners suggest their ideas (walking, standing, looking at a map, smiling, eating a mango, holding an ear, filming the jungle). Write these verbs and phrases on the board. Some learners mime a verb that is on the board. Others guess which one they are miming.

Test tip: MOVERS
Speaking Part 1

✔ Learners see eight or nine people in the picture and also seven possible names. When they listen, they will only hear about six of the people in the picture and have to use six of the names (one of which is the example).

➜ Before learners do this task, train them to quickly, but also carefully, look at each person in the picture and notice what they are doing or wearing/holding or where they are in the picture, as this is the kind of information they will need to understand to be able to name them correctly.

- Ask *How many names can you see outside the picture?* (six) *Which are girls' names?* (Anna, Lucy, Grace, sometimes also Charlie) *Which are boys' names?* (Paul, Matt, Charlie)

- Ask *How many grown-ups can you see?* (two)

- Say *Listen to the girl. She's talking to her uncle about five of these people. What are their names?* Explain in L1 that they won't hear the name of one of the people in the picture.

- Play the audio twice. Do the example. Pause the audio after *Now you listen and draw lines.* Learners point to the line between *Grace* and the girl with a parrot on her shoulder. They then listen and draw lines. Check answers in open class.

20

Tapescript:

Girl: I'm reading a story about the jungle, Uncle Pat. Look at this picture.

Man: It's great. Are these people going for a walk?

Girl: Yes! There's Grace.

Man: The girl with the parrot on her shoulder?

Girl: That's right. She's wearing her new yellow shorts.

Can you see the line? This is an example.

Now you listen and draw lines.

1 Man: What's that boy doing? The boy in the blue jeans.

Girl: He's filming the jungle.

Man: Oh! Exciting! What's his name?

Girl: Charlie. He loves jungles. He's looking for jungle animals, I think.

Man: Great!

2 Man: And who's the little girl with long brown hair?

Girl: She's called Lucy. She's got her teddy bear with her.

Man: Does she always have that with her?

Girl: Not always, but sometimes.

3 Girl: And there's Paul.

Man: The boy eating a mango?

Girl: No. The grown-up with the map.

Man: Oh! Where are they going?

Girl: I don't know!

4 Man: What's the woman's name?

Girl: That's Anna.

Man: Why is she holding her ear? Is there a fly in her ear?

Girl: No! She's got earache.

Man: Oh dear!

Girl: Don't worry! She's OK. She gets better after the walk.

Answers

Learners draw lines between:
Charlie – boy filming
Lucy – girl with teddy bear
Paul – man with map
Anna – woman with earache

J Complete your story.

- Say *Now let's write a story about the jungle. Complete the sentences.*

- Learners use their imagination. They work on their own and then read their text to their friend.

7   *Let's have fun!*

Colour the map and write about three animals that live there.

Give learners Photocopy 7 (TB page 59). Ask *Can you see the rainforests on the map? Colour them green.* Then ask *Now what do you need to find out?* Learners think about what to type into an internet search engine. Ask *Which animals live in rainforests?* Learners look for pictures of animals.

Write questions on the board: *What is it called? Where does it live? What colour is it? Is it big or small? How many legs has it got? What can it do?* Learners research their animals online and then write a short paragraph about them. Learners can look at page 71, Activity 7, for an example paragraph about a parrot. You can display their work in the classroom.

7   *Let's speak!*

What's the matter? Ask and answer.

Tell learners to look at page 73, Activity 7. Demonstrate the conversation with one learner, asking *Have you got earache?* (Yes, I have.) Then mime having stomach-ache, by holding your stomach. Gesture to indicate that students need to ask you the question *Have you got stomach-ache?* Respond *Yes, I have.*

Mime other illnesses, such as toothache and headache. Learners ask you more *Have you got … ?* questions. Learners continue asking and answering in pairs.

29

◄)) *Let's say!* Page 75
Say *Look at page 75. Listen.* Play the audio. Say *Let's say /æ/ man, fat.* Learners repeat. Say *Tell me more English words with /æ/.* Learners answer (e.g. apple, Gran, alphabet). Repeat with sound /ʌ/ (e.g. uncle, drum). Learners listen again to the audio, repeating the rhyme as fast as they can.

Home FUN booklet
➡ **Pages 18–19**
➡ **Picture dictionary: health, world around us**

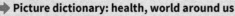

Go online
to practise your English to listen to the audio recordings to find more FUN activities!

Henry's holiday

8

Main topics:	sport and leisure
Story summary:	Henry goes on holiday with his family, but he prefers staying at home. They have lots of problems and Henry suggests a solution.
Main grammar:	verb + infinitive (*want to*), have (got) to, like / doesn't like
Main vocabulary:	*blanket, cheese, countryside, drop, exciting, field, film, ground, headache, holiday, hurt, parents, place, rain, Saturday, shark, snail, snow, soup, Sunday, terrible, weather, wet, windy*
Value:	Finding solutions to problems ("*I know! I can …*")
Let's say!:	/ɪ/, /iː/
Practice for Movers:	Speaking Part 2 (C), Listening Part 4 (F), Reading and Writing Part 3 (G), Speaking Part 1 (H)

Equipment:	
	• audio: Story, F • ⟶ presentation **PLUS** flashcards Go to Presentation plus to find pictures of Movers vocabulary from Unit 8. You can use the pictures to teach/review important words in this unit.	• ⟶ presentation **PLUS** Image carousel 55–57 (pictures of beach, mountains, camping): Storytelling • crayons or colouring pens: Let's have fun! • Photocopy 8 (TB page 60): Storytelling

---

⭐📖 Storytelling

Before listening

With books closed …

- Introduce the topic of the story. Ask learners about their holidays: *Where do you like going on holiday? Do you like going to the beach? The mountains? The city? The countryside?* Say *This story is about a boy. His name is Henry. Henry goes on holiday with his parents.*
- Show photographs of people on holiday from the Image carousel. Ask *What can you see? What are they doing?* Learners answer, e.g. *They are walking in the mountains. They are sitting on a beach.*
- Ask *Where do you stay on holiday?* Accept lots of ideas and then review/teach *tent*. Draw a picture of yourself in a tent. Say *This is me in my tent.* Draw a blanket and a torch. Say *This is my blanket and this is my torch.* Ask *What do you do in a tent?* (sleep) *When do you need a torch?* (at night)
- Learners look at the first picture without the story text on the Image carousel or with the story text in the book on page 60. Ask *Who's this?* (Henry / a boy) *What's he holding?* (a torch) *Where is he?* (in the kitchen) *What does Henry want to eat?* (learners guess – ice cream)
- Say *Now let's listen to the story.* Say *Let's look at page 60.*

Listening

With books open …

21

- Play the audio or read the story. Learners listen.
- Play the audio or read the story again.
- Pause after '*…and no TV. I want to go home!*' on page 61. Ask *Where are the family now?* (in the countryside) *Is there a television?* (no) *Is Henry happy?* (no) *What does Henry want to do?* (go home)
- Pause after '*Can we go home now, Mum?*' *he asked* on page 61. Ask *Does Henry want to help his parents?* (no) *Is it sunny now?* (no – it's raining) *What is wet now?* (the blankets)
- At the end of the story, ask *Did the family have a good dinner?* (no) Teach *snore* by making the noise. Learners make snoring sounds too for fun.
- Ask *Who snored in the night?* (Henry's dad/father) *Were Henry and his parents happy the next morning?* (no) *Where are they going at the end of the story?* (home)

After listening

- Say *Close your eyes. Imagine Henry's perfect holiday. What does he do? Where does he go?* Learners suggest ideas. Give each learner a copy of Photocopy 8 (TB page 60). Say *What does Henry do on holiday at home? Imagine. Read and tick.* Learners decide which activities Henry likes doing. Say *Now continue the story. Write about Henry's perfect day.* Learners use the phrases they ticked to help them. Walk around and check that learners are using the past tense. Learners can read their completed stories to their friend.

A. Read and complete the words.

- Learners look at the example and then, in pairs, read the definitions and complete the words. Check answers in open class. Ask learners to spell the word, e.g. *Which animal has a shell on its back?* (a snail) *How do you spell it?* (S-N-A-I-L) Check pronunciation.
- Draw attention to the /ʃ/ sound in <u>shoulders</u> and <u>shower</u>. Ask learners for other words they know with this sound (e.g. shop, sheep, ship, shell, shirt).

Answers

2 snail **3** comic **4** shoulders **5** shower **6** soup

B. Read and circle the correct answer.

- Learners look at the example. Ask *Why is there a circle around 'doesn't like'?* (because Henry doesn't like holidays)
- Learners read sentences 2–5 and, in pairs, choose and circle the right answer in pencil.

Answers

2 countryside **3** Sunday **4** badly **5** lizard

- Write two questions on the board:

  What do you do on Saturdays?

  Do you like going to the countryside or to the beach?

- Ask one or two learners the questions in open class. Then learners ask and answer the questions in pairs.
- Divide learners into groups of three or four. Draw a lizard and a spider on the board. Ask *What's the difference between a lizard and a spider? How many legs has a lizard got? How many has a spider got?* Give groups two minutes to think about other differences. The group with the most ideas wins the task.

Suggested answers

Lizards	Spiders
are grey or green	are black or brown (usually)
have feet and a tail	don't have feet or a tail
eat fruit	don't eat fruit

C. Look at the pictures. Tell the story with words from the box.

- Say *Look at the first picture. Who can you see?* (Henry) *Where is he?* (in bed) *What is he doing?* (reading a comic) Point to the last picture and say *This is the last picture.* Ask *Where's Henry?* (in the car) *Where are the family going?* (home) Say *Use the words in the box to say sentences about the other pictures. Tell the story.*
- In pairs, the learners talk about all four pictures.
- Walk around and offer help.
- Ask a few pairs to tell their story in open class.

Suggested answers

Henry is reading a comic.
Henry and his mum and dad are in a tent. It's cold. They are eating soup.
It's night. Henry's mum and dad are sleeping. Henry isn't sleeping!
They are in the car now. They are driving. They are going home.

Test tip: MOVERS
Speaking – All parts

- ✔ Learners need to complete four tasks. Make sure they are familiar with the order of tasks and what they will need to do so they feel as confident as possible. They may want to ask the examiner to repeat an instruction. Tell learners it is fine to do that.
- → Practise using greetings and leavings and asking for clarification or a repeated instruction, e.g. *Sorry! I don't understand. Sorry! Can you say that again?* Knowing it's fine to talk in this way will reassure learners they will be helped if necessary.

D. Draw lines to the correct box.

- Ask *What do you like doing?* Put learners' first three suggestions on the board, e.g. *(Alex) likes playing football.*
- Ask *What don't you like doing?* Put the first three suggestions on the board too, e.g. *(Maria) doesn't like doing homework.*
- Learners look at the activities on the board. Different learners each mime an activity to check understanding. Other learners guess what they are doing.
- Ask *Can you remember one thing that Henry likes doing? And one thing that Henry doesn't like doing?* Write their answers on the board.
- In pairs, learners now draw lines connecting each of these activities under the '*Henry likes*' or '*Henry doesn't like*' headings in the table. Learners may have to look at page 60 of the story or at the pictures to do this. Pairs do this as quickly as they can and tell you when they have finished.
- Check answers. Ask *Does Henry like eating ice cream?* (yes) *Does Henry like going on holiday?* (no)

Answers

Henry likes: eating ice cream, listening to music, watching television, having hot showers, finding snails, reading comics, having hot dinners

Henry doesn't like: going on holiday, going for long walks, sleeping in a tent, having sand in his socks

E Read and write.

- Learners read the example. Ask *What's wrong?* (it's raining) *What can Henry do?* (put on a hat and coat and run to school)
- Teach useful phrases. Ask *What do we say when we have a problem?* (Oh no!) *What can we say when we have an idea?* (I know! I can …) Write these phrases on the board.
- Put learners into groups of three or four. They read sentences 1–4 and think about things they could do in each case. Walk around and help with vocabulary if necessary. Learners perform short role plays for each scenario. Groups do their role play for the class, suggesting solutions for each problem.

Suggested answers

1 I know! I can make a hot drink. I can have a hot shower. I can find a blanket.

2 I know! I can make a sandwich. I can buy some chocolate. I can ask a friend to give me some of his/her food.

3 I know! I can sit down. I can go to sleep. I can stop walking. I can find something to eat and drink. I can catch a bus home.

4 I know! I can phone the doctor. I can go to bed. I can lie down on the sofa. I can drink lots of water.

F Listen and tick (✔) the box.

- Review/Teach *forget*. Say *I'm going to see my friend. I want to take my camera, my toothbrush, an apple, my pen and my sunglasses with me.*
- Mime putting things in a bag and say *Here's my apple, my sunglasses, my toothbrush and my pen. Good!* Ask *What did I forget to put in my bag?* (your camera!) Ask *What do you sometimes forget to put in your school bag?*
- Learners look at the 12 pictures. Ask *In which picture can you see this?* and write on the board: *map, towel, sandwich, toothbrush.* In pairs, learners write down the number and letter of the picture which shows each thing.

Suggested answers:

map – 1C   towel – 1B   sandwich – 4C   toothbrush – 1A

- Learners read the four questions.

22

- Play the audio. Pause after the first question and look at the example. Play the rest of the audio. Learners listen and tick the correct boxes.

Tapescript:

1   What didn't Dad take on holiday?

   Dad: I brought the towels, Henry. Here!

   Henry: Cool!

   Dad: But I didn't bring our toothbrushes!

   Henry: Oh no!

   Dad: Well, we can buy some new ones.
   And here's the map, Henry. Don't lose it!

2   What's in Mum's bag?

   Mum: Aaagh! Come and help me, Henry. There's an animal in my bag!

   Henry: What is it, Mum? A mouse?

   Mum: No, and it's not a lizard.

   Henry: It's only a frog, Mum! Don't be afraid!

3   Where's Henry's kite now?

   Dad: Where's your kite, Henry? Is that it? On the grass?

   Henry: No. It's in the car, Dad.

   Dad: Well, go and get it. Then put it in the tent.

   Henry: OK!

4   What's for breakfast?

   Henry: What's for breakfast, Mum? Sausages?

   Mum: We can't have those, Henry, but we can have some sandwiches.

   Henry: Can we have eggs too? I love those.

   Mum: Me too, but no. Sorry, Henry! We haven't got any.

Answers

2 B   **3** A   **4** C

- Ask *Who didn't bring the toothbrushes?* (Henry's father) *Who was afraid?* (Henry's mother) *Who's got a kite?* (Henry) *Who wants eggs for breakfast?* (Henry and his mother)

G Complete the sentences. Write 1 or 2 words.

- Learners look at the example. Ask *How many words are in the answer?* (one) *How many words can you write in an answer?* (one or two)
- In pairs, learners find the answers and write them on the dotted lines.

Answers

2 tablet   **3** Henry   **4** woke   **5** bad headache   **6** lizard

- Ask *How many times did Henry wake up?* (forty-two!)

H Look at the picture on page 63. Find eight differences.

- Learners look at the top picture on page 63. Ask *Is it the night or the morning now?* (the morning) *Are Henry and his parents happy?* (no)
- Learners also look at the picture in Activity H. Say *Some things in the two pictures are different. In this picture* (point to the picture on page 63) *it's cloudy. But in this picture* (page 66) *it's …* (sunny)
- Write this model on the board:

   In this picture it's cloudy, but in this picture it's sunny.

   Practise this in open class and leave it on the board.

- Talk about one more difference. A pair of learners complete another sentence: *In this picture the tent is green, but in this picture it's …* (purple)
- In pairs or small groups, learners find six other differences and think how to describe them. Walk round, helping with language if necessary. Groups take turns to tell the class one difference.

Test tip: MOVERS
Speaking Part 1

✔ Learners have to spot and explain five differences between two pictures. These may relate to, e.g. colour, number, size, position, activity, time and weather.

➔ Use any picture to practise identifying these details. Ask *What colour, Which is bigger/smaller, Where, What doing, When, What/like* questions.

I Read and complete the story. Choose a word from the box.

- Learners read the text without completing it. Ask *What colour is this animal?* (green) *Is it big or small?* (small) Ask *Do you like lizards?*

- Learners complete the text, using words from the box. Encourage them to cross words out after they have used them. Note there is one extra word.

Answers

2 spiders   **3** legs   **4** crocodile   **5** rained   **6** sleeping

- Ask *Do you like hot, sunny weather? Do crocodiles like hot, sunny weather? Which other animals like hot, sunny weather?*

- Pairs list animals they know that live in hot, sunny places. Each pair chooses one of their animals. The rest of the class guesses which animal they have chosen. They ask, e.g. *What colour is it? How many legs has it got?*

Suggested answers

Starters words:	elephant, giraffe, hippo, monkey, snake, tiger, crocodile, lizard, zebra
Movers words:	kangaroo, lion

Extension

Learners find pictures in magazines, comics, etc. of animals that like hot, sunny weather. They cut them out and make a poster, adding the animals' names and where they live. Display the posters around the classroom.

J Read and write the days under the correct pictures.

- Ask *What's the weather like today? It's cloudy/nice/ hot/cold.* Explain that *like* here looks the same as *like* in *I like ice cream*, but has a very different meaning.

- Ask more questions: *What's your flat like? What's your school like?* Learners answer using *It's* + adjective.

- Review/Teach the days of the week. Show that in English the names of the days of the week begin with a capital letter, like names for boys and girls.

- Practise the days of the week.

- Ask *What day was it yesterday? What day is it today?* Two learners write these days on the board.

- Point out that we say *on* a day. Say a sentence about yourself, using *on* and a day.

- Learners read Henry's diary and write the correct day under each picture.

- Check the answers in open class.

Answers

1 Saturday   **2** Sunday   **3** Monday   **4** Friday

8 *Let's have fun!*

Do a weather project for this week. Make a poster.

Ask *What was the weather like on Henry's holiday? Was it sunny?* (no) *Did it rain?* (yes) *Did it snow?* (no) *Was it windy?* (yes)

Ask *What's the weather like today? Is it hot? Is it windy? Is it cloudy? What can you do in this weather?*

Learners look at the chart in Activity 8 on page 71 and draw a similar chart on a large piece of paper.

They write and draw the weather and write the temperature every day this week, next to the correct day, as in the example for Monday.

Complete the chart for a week, at the end of the school day. Learners write a short sentence saying what the weather was like that day.

At the end of the week, ask *How many days were sunny? How many days were cold? Did it snow? Did you see a rainbow? Did you like the weather?*

Display these weather projects around the classroom if possible.

8 *Let's speak!*

What do you like doing on holiday? Ask and answer.

Tell learners to look at page 73, Activity 8. Read the examples together.

Ask *What do you like doing on holiday?* Demonstrate with a strong learner.

Ask *What about you? Ask and answer.*

Ask a pair of confident learners to perform their conversation for the class.

 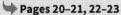

30 ◀)) *Let's say!* **Page 75**

Say *Look at page 75. Listen.* Play the audio. Say *Let's say* /ɪ/ *little, kitchen.* Learners repeat.
Say *Tell me more English words with* /ɪ/. Learners answer (e.g. it, internet, invite). Repeat with sound /iː/ (e.g. easy, week).
Learners listen again to the audio, repeating the rhyme as fast as they can.

Home FUN booklet

➥ **Pages 20–21, 22–23**
➥ **Picture dictionary: sports and leisure, weather**

Go online

to practise your English
to listen to the audio recordings
to find more FUN activities!

An animal poster

Draw and write about an animal.

It lives in …		
It's got	two / four / six	legs. arms. eyes.
It's a	furry / dangerous / noisy / quiet	animal.
It's got a	big / small / long / short / fat	body. tail.
It eats …		

....

....

....

....

....

....

Story characters

2

Match the characters and what they say. Draw lines.

Today we went to the funfair. We met an alien called Jog! He was very kind. We went for a ride in his spaceship! It was cool!

Jog

Today I went to the hospital with Miss Read. Outside, I saw an alien! I'm afraid of aliens. Miss Read said it was Mr Doors, but it wasn't!

Mr Doors

Today I went to the bookshop with Mrs Doors. We saw Charlie in the supermarket, wearing funny clothes. Mrs Doors said he was an alien! How silly!

Lily

Today I went to Skiptown. I went to the supermarket, to the car park and to the circus. Then I went to the funfair.

Miss Kite

Today I went to the town centre with Charlie. We drove the truck. We saw Miss Kite in the car park in her new hat. Charlie said she was an alien! How funny!

Sam and Julia

Good friends

3

1 What's a good friend? Tick (✓) the ideas which are most important for you.

Good friends are funny. ☐

Good friends like animals. ☐

Good friends are clever. ☐

Good friends like sport. ☐

Good friends are happy. ☐

Good friends like music. ☐

Good friends are my age. ☐

Good friends have cool clothes. ☐

2 Make new friends! Do a survey.

	My answer	Person with the same answer
Favourite band?	....	....
Favourite sport?	....	....
Favourite animal?	....	....
Favourite hobby?	....	....
Favourite school subject?	....	....
Favourite book?	....	....

A sports poster

1 Draw a picture of your sport.

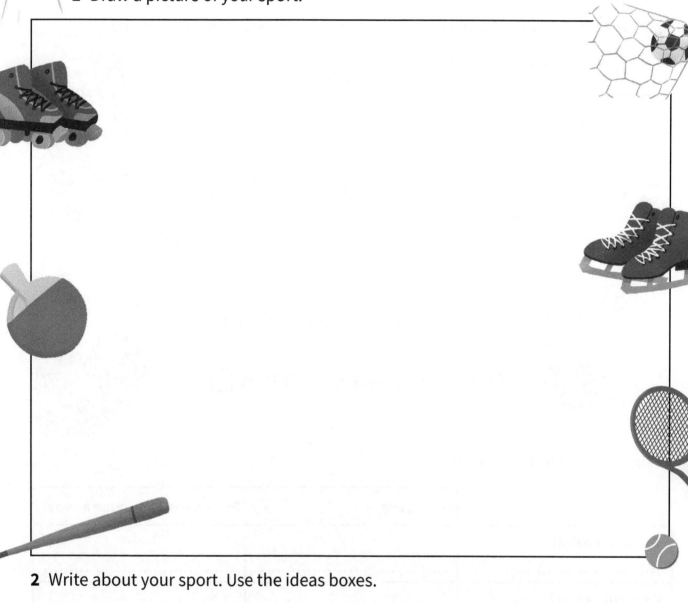

2 Write about your sport. Use the ideas boxes.

What equipment do you need?
ball   bat   racket   net   swimming pool
How many players do you need?

Are you good at this sport?
Would you like to try this sport?
Where can you play this sport?
Is it easy / difficult / exciting / dangerous?

....
....
....
....
....

5 The monster under my bed!

What's the title of the story?

Where does the story happen?

What's the problem?
There's a .... under the ....

Who are the characters?

What happens at the end of the story?
The girl .... under the ....
It isn't a ...., it's a .... !

I like this story. ☐
I don't like this story. ☐

Our survey

always ✱ often ✱ sometimes ✱ never

Our names: ....

	always	often	sometimes	never
I get up at seven o'clock.				
I have lunch at one o'clock.				
I go to bed before eleven o'clock.				

I walk to school.				
I come to school by bus.				
I fly to school in our helicopter.				

I play volleyball with my friends.				
I play football on the beach.				
I play table tennis at the sports centre.				

I read in the bath.				
I draw on a computer at weekends.				
I watch DVDs at home.				

Rainforest animals

Colour the rainforests. Now write about three animals that live in rainforests.

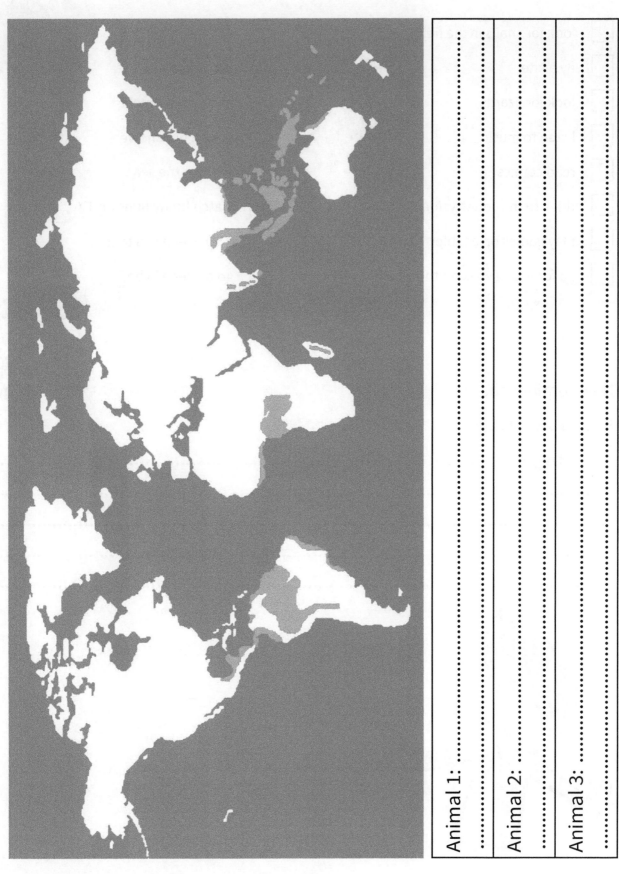

Animal 1: ....

Animal 2: ....

Animal 3: ....

Henry's holiday

What does Henry do on holiday at home? Read and tick (✓).

- [ ] look for snails in the field
- [ ] fly a kite
- [ ] look for lizards
- [ ] listen to music
- [ ] read comics
- [ ] drive to the countryside
- [ ] play games on a tablet
- [ ] go for a long walk on the beach

- [ ] eat ice cream
- [ ] eat cold soup
- [ ] have a hot dinner
- [ ] have a hot shower
- [ ] swim in the sea
- [ ] watch funny films on TV
- [ ] go to sleep in a tent
- [ ] go to sleep in bed

Now continue the story.

Henry's perfect day

The next day Henry got up at eight o'clock. He ....

....

....

....

....

STORYFUN 3

To: ....

Name of school: ....

Date: ....

Signed: ....

Well done!

Audio track listing

01	Title and copyright
02	Jack and the penguins
03	Jack and the penguins I
04	Jog the alien
05	Jog the alien E
06	Jog the alien I
07	My friend Meg
08	My friend Meg F
09	My friend Meg I
10	High five!
11	High five! F
12	High five! I
13	The monster under my bed
14	The monster under my bed G
15	The monster under my bed J
16	What a great grandmother!
17	What a great grandmother! K
18	The old man and the jungle
19	The old man and the jungle G
20	The old man and the jungle I
21	Henry's holiday
22	Henry's holiday F
23	Let's say! 1
24	Let's say! 2
25	Let's say! 3
26	Let's say! 4
27	Let's say! 5
28	Let's say! 6
29	Let's say! 7
30	Let's say! 8
31	Karaoke song – The circus
32	Karaoke song – At Treetop Park

Acknowledgements

The author would like to acknowledge the shared professionalism and FUN she's experienced whilst working with colleagues during 20 years of production of YLE tests. She would also like to thank CUP for their support in the writing of this second edition of Storyfun.

On a personal note, Karen fondly thanks her inspirational story-telling grandfather, and now, three generations later, her sons, Tom and Will, for adding so much creative fun to our continuation of the family story-telling and story-making tradition.

The author and publishers would like to thank the following ELT professionals who commented on the material at different stages of development: Louise Manicolo, Mexico; Mandy Watkins, Greece.

Design and typeset by Wild Apple Design.

Cover design and header artwork by Nicholas Jackson (Astound). Sound recordings by Hart McLeod, Cambridge.

Music by Mark Fishlock and produced by Ian Harker. Recorded at The Soundhouse Studios, London. The authors and publishers acknowledge the following sources of copyright material and are grateful for the permissions granted. While every effort has been made, it has not always been possible to identify the sources of all the material used, or to trace all copyright holders. If any omissions are brought to our notice, we will be happy to include the appropriate acknowledgements on reprinting.

The authors and publishers are grateful to the following illustrators:

Key: BL = Bottom Left; TL = Top Left; TR = Top Right.

Chiara Buccheri c/o Lemonade p. 57
Nigel Dobbyn c/o Beehive Illustration p. 59
Bonnie Pang c/o Astound pp. 56, 61 (TL)
Esther Pérez-Cuadrado c/o Beehive Illustration p. 61
Melanie Sharp c/o Sylvie Poggio Artist agency p. 60
Simon Smith c/o Beehive Illustration pp. 54, 61, (TR)
Sarah Warburton pp. 55, 61 (BL)
Cherie Zamazing p. 61

DID YOU KNOW CAMBRIDGE ENGLISH: YOUNG LEARNERS (YLE) IS UPDATING IN 2018?

VISIT **WORLD OF FUN** ONLINE FOR:

| Information about the 2018 test changes | Tips and resources for teaching Young Learners | Official materials to prepare for the updated tests |

www.cambridge.org/worldoffun